Tears of a Clown

My story of domestic violence

Leena Derham

BALMORAL
BEACH
PRESS

Tears of a Clown
First published by Balmoral Beach Press, 2021

Copyright © 2021 Leena Derham

Book design by Balmoral Beach Press
www.balmoralbeach.press

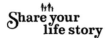 

Contents

Author's note

My life isn't over, but it's time my story was told. In no way do I believe my story of love and loss outranks anyone else's, but I feel compelled to share it to prevent others from experiencing the depth of despair I have endured throughout most of my life.

I often think of my life as footprints in the sand— some will wash away and disappear, but I'll never forget them. Some will remain deeply embedded and others will scatter, blown away by the wind.

Several people have told me I am an inspiration to them and that my journey might reach others who are going through a similar situation. I don't feel I'm worthy of such a pedestal. Still, if my story touches one person and helps them, that will be enough for me.

For most of my life, I felt suppressed. I wasn't allowed to openly talk about problems or express emotions, and I was told to harden up and get on with it. It's now my life's mission to teach my kids and others that it is okay to not be okay. It is okay to cry. Never be afraid and be true to yourself. We are all individuals and yes, we come with flaws, but we shouldn't be made to feel judged because our personality shape doesn't perfectly fit another person's view of how we should be.

Every footprint marked my journey to this point in my life, and I am now ready to share it with you, hoping I can save you from the many mistakes that have landed me where I am today. I long to prevent what happened to me from happening to you.

Prologue

It is Friday 29 January 2021, a sunny, warm summer morning. I can hear the lorikeets chirping in the front garden and my two children chatting excitedly. It was my son Daniel's birthday four days ago and he and his younger sister Sophie are trying out his new gadgets.

My mobile phone rings—one, two, three rings. I freeze when I notice Tom's name pop up on the screen. The name of the man I loved for 13 years. The man who fathered my beautiful son and daughter. The man who could make me feel loved and secure only to shatter the core of my being a moment later.

The phone keeps ringing, but my head is still spinning from the tirade I just read in Tom's latest email. Full of hatred and vitriol, he blames me for everything that has gone wrong in our lives. Tom, my partner and the man of my dreams, threatened to destroy me. I fear he means it. With little regard for the law, he breached last week's family violence intervention order. I don't think I will ever be able to trust him again. I believe nothing he says because of his continual lies that have recently become fanciful and larger than life. Refusing to get help, he believes everyone else is the problem, not him.

A few weeks ago, Tom told me he knows how to hide

a body because he watches all the crime investigation shows on television then laughed it off to make it seem like he was joking, I wasn't convinced. He told his sister he can fool anyone, no matter how smart they are. I fear for my life.

Every time I leave the house, I glance over my shoulder, checking for danger. I do the same at home too. I don't feel safe anywhere and live on the adrenaline of the fight-or-flight response. No matter where I go in Australia, I know Tom will find me and my children. I tried so hard to give Daniel a fabulous birthday and took him to his favourite restaurant with his friends, but I knew Tom was hovering somewhere nearby. I worried Tom was watching us as we celebrated. It was intensely stressful, and I felt sorry for Daniel that this was dampening the excitement of his tenth birthday, which is such an important milestone in a young boy's life. I desperately wanted Daniel to see his father but was advised not to by the police.

The phone keeps ringing—four, five, six rings. I feel paralysed, unable to press the green button that will unleash another torrent of malice. After enduring more than a decade of vicious battering, something in me has broken. I am numb. I don't want to speak to him or listen to his venomous diatribe anymore.

I thrust my mobile phone into my friend's hands. Deep furrows form in her brow, but she answers it.

'Can I speak to Leena, please,' Tom says, putting on his politest voice, a voice calm and in control.

I shake my head, the tears of a clown welling up in my eyes.

'No Tom, no,' my friend says, shaking her head and hanging up on him.

Next, the house phone rings. I feel the knot in the pit of my stomach tighten.

What would have happened if I had answered? Why did he not let the thought of what he was about to do to the kids stop him? He must have been in the darkest place. Could talking to him have stopped him from doing what he did? Would he have done it while on the phone to me?

Growing up

I wish I could look back on my childhood and say it was filled with love, security and happiness. Some of it was, most of it was not. I realised from about the age of six that my mother had a drinking problem. Being an only child, I was acutely aware of Mum's behaviour because I didn't have the distraction of a sibling. Dad would try to protect me, but I saw things a child should not see.

I was born in England to English parents and our extended family lived there. When I was four going on five, we moved to Africa for Dad's job. I can't remember where Dad was, but Mum and I were staying in a hotel. One night I suddenly woke up and saw a strange man lying on top of Mum. He was moving up and down and grunting. I screamed at him to get off and leave Mum alone, but he ignored me. My screaming must have panicked him because he soon got up and left the room. Mum didn't respond to my cries, and I had no-one else to turn to. I had never felt so scared. This memory is etched in my mind forever.

From about eight years old, my mother's drinking skyrocketed. Displaying alcohol was never an option in our home, so Dad locked up his supply in the spare bedroom. Mum couldn't access alcohol at home, but an addict will always source what they need, and she was no exception. She'd knock on the doors of friends and family looking for some liquid nectar.

Mum also sold our treasured possessions to fund her alcohol purchases. If Dad didn't nail it down or lock it up, Mum would have sold or traded it for a bottle of something alcoholic. It broke Dad's heart because she sold her wedding ring, jewellery and many other valuable treasures.

An intoxicated mother became my normal, and I cherished the rare moments when Mum was sober. Those happy times of singing together and playing hide and seek are forever etched in my memory. But playtime didn't last long, and Mum soon returned to her inebriated state. Being an only child, it was up to me to make my own entertainment, and there were many times when I felt alone and abandoned. Fortunately, I felt loved by my father, who was really my stepfather, which helped to ease the pain. I saw more and heard more than the average child and grew into an adult way of thinking at a young age. I felt guilty, as if it were my fault that Mum was an alcoholic. Maybe if I behaved better, she would stop drinking? Maybe if I helped her more, she would stop drinking? Maybe if I did better at school…

These questions buzzed inside my head like bees around a honeypot. I felt it was up to me to save Mum. But how? In some respects, I was robbed of a childhood, but my dad tried his best to make up for Mum's behaviour. I adored him.

My school day started at 7:30 am and finished at 12:30 pm. Dad would pick me up, take me home, and we would eat lunch with Mum. But that pattern abruptly stopped when I turned eight. Dad would take me home at midday, but the house would often be empty. The lunch Mum usually pre-prepared was missing, and we couldn't find her anywhere. We checked every room and searched for a note, but we couldn't find Mum or a note explaining where she was. We waited and waited, and Dad would take the afternoon off work so he could search the local area. Dad and I would drive around, checking in all the bowling clubs, golf clubs and bars. 'Have you seen my mum?' I'd ask the patrons, but they all shook their heads.

During her absences, Mum didn't telephone us, and we had no way of knowing if she was safe... or even alive. Dad and I would call the hospitals, even the mortuary, which at eight years old was terrifying. Most of the time, Mum would return three or four weeks later, looking worse for wear. When she arrived home, I was so relieved I didn't question her, afraid it might trigger another unexplained departure. Thank God, I thought. She's home and we can have a normal life again. I was quick to ignore Mum's betrayal, just to feel like a normal kid with a mother and father at home. I didn't want to worry about what might happen tomorrow, instead focusing on today.

Every time Mum returned home, I worried about the way Dad bombarded her with questions. She refused to answer them, and my parent's arguments continued for days. I knew these quarrels would make Mum leave us again. Out of frustration Dad sometimes hit Mum or pushed her. 'Get out, get out,' he would shout at the top of his voice. I'd be nearby and hear it. I quivered, hoping Mum would stay with us but knowing in my bones that she would soon flee.

'Focus on the fact that she's home now,' I'd say to Dad, urging him to calm his rage and treat Mum with kid gloves. But the hurt and the anger he felt was so consuming, his tolerance was diminishing at a fast rate. Mum reassured me she wouldn't run away again, but she did, many, many times.

After school I sometimes invited a friend home. But several times when my friend and I walked through the front door, the house was empty. It was quiet and still, and I instinctively knew Mum had done another runner. It embarrassed me. 'Oh, I forgot my mum has a dentist's appointment,' I'd lie. That's when the lies started. I learned that from Dad because he said that even family members were never to be told about what Mum was doing.

Sometimes as I sat watching television, I would notice Mum had disappeared. When she returned an hour or so later, I instinctively knew she was drunk. I begged Mum to stop drinking, but to no avail. I yearned for her to stop drinking and thought if I showered her with love and was always on my best behaviour, she would give up alcohol and we could be a normal family. I tried to capture as many sober moments as possible, and cherished them, hoping they would last forever. But at the back of my mind, I always had a nagging doubt these precious times were fleeting. I knew Mum loved me, but I also knew deep down that her love was not enough to stop her addiction or keep her close to me.

Mum was slim because she ate so little. Whenever she did eat, I felt excited and relieved, hoping it would reduce her need for alcohol. She often made me soft-boiled eggs with buttered soldiers, and she loved cracking off the top of the egg.

'Eat it,' I'd plead. 'Please eat it.' I thought if Mum ate, she would grow stronger and that would mean she would stop drinking.

My mother couldn't give me what I needed as a child because of her alcoholism. I sensed that she loved me, but she loved alcohol more. Sometimes she showed flickers of determination and I sensed that she realised what she was doing to herself and her family. But they were momentary. Still, I never gave up hope. As a child, your parents are your everything. You hope that if you love them that much harder, it will light the flame to fight the battle. I would beg Mum to see beyond the bottle and that she was missing out on so much, with so much to live for.

One day, I started sobbing. Mum asked me what was wrong, so I told her I was scared of her dying. She assured me she wasn't going anywhere. No child wants to lose their parent, and no parent wants to lose their child, something that now haunts me.

As a child my wild imagination helped me create

entertainment for myself to distract me from my loneliness and the realities of a wretched home life. One thing I loved to do was to put a pillow under my top or dress and pretend I was pregnant. I would even walk around with my hand at the base of my lower back, pretending to support the enormous belly. For as long as I can remember, I always longed for children, and I made a vow to my unborn babies that I would always be there for them. I wanted them to feel confident they could rely on me and trust me to always be there for them. I promised to do my utmost to never let them down. Little did I know then how that promise would be broken, no matter how vigorously I struggled to keep it.

Travelling abroad on my own

Growing up, I fell in love with Enid Blyton's books for children. Malory Towers, a series of six novels about life at a girls' boarding school, captivated me. It sounded so exciting, fun filled and innocent. My best memory at primary school was reading time in the library. I would rush to my spot under a table in the library and devour boarding school adventures such as midnight feasts with lashings of lemonade. Enid Blyton's books fuelled my wild imagination and took me to places far away from the gloomy realities of my home life. They were my welcome escape.

One day when I was about 10, I was chatting with Dad, and I blurted out the idea of me going to boarding school. I told him about the Malory Towers stories and how I loved the idea of going to a boarding school. I thought nothing would come out of it, but the casual chat soon turned an idea into a possibility. Before I knew it, my parents were applying to schools. They had decided it would be good for me. Mock-entrance exams soon started arriving in the post and I had to embark on a strict study schedule that I hated with a passion. I spent hours upon hours with Dad sitting at the dining room table learning my times tables and spelling. And yes, there were a few, well, a lot of tears, especially over maths.

After what seemed forever, a boarding school in England accepted me. It wasn't Malory Towers, but it was still boarding school. The excitement of so much imagined fun with my new chums overwhelmed me. When I turned 11, I travelled to England to start my adventure.

Fast track a few weeks in my new home and it was nothing like I thought it would be. Being away from my parents and living in a different country pushed me out of my comfort zone. At heart, I was a bush girl who had enjoyed all the freedom of the world, so suddenly finding myself alone in a strict school regimen in a country I didn't know was confronting. Fortunately, I could visit my grandparents every couple of weekends, but that didn't make up for not having Mum and Dad with me. Dad wrote to me every week, and he included little drawings of daily life at home. They were bad drawings, but I treasure them and still keep them in a box. Dad used to draw me pictures of what my cat Tom was doing with Kerry, my dog, and he'd draw terrible but funny pictures of them watching television together. I used to look forward to receiving them and spent all week wondering what Dad would draw next time.

Sadly, Dad's letters didn't quell my homesickness. Each term was an interminable 12 weeks, and I ached to see my parents. My longing was overwhelming and as the end of term grew closer, my excitement grew. So did the bulkiness of my suitcase as I added gifts and goodies to take home to Mum and Dad.

At the beginning of the school holidays, I'd fly home to see my parents. When my plane landed, my heart raced with excitement. It was the best feeling, almost as good as waking up on Christmas morning excited to see if Father Christmas had been. Waiting for my suitcase in baggage claim was agonising because the conveyer belt was excruciatingly slow, and my bag seemed to be at the end of the line. When I spotted my bulky suitcase, my spirits soared. Once through customs, I ran through the terminal to find my parents.

Scanning the crowd, I quickly spotted Dad, because he stood head and shoulders above everyone else. Then my eyes settled on the place next to Dad, but sometimes Mum wasn't there. I searched through the hundreds of people crammed into the terminal, but I couldn't see Mum. My heart sank, and tears streamed down my face. I tried to lock eyes with Dad, but he glanced away. I could see by the look on his face that Mum wasn't there. He knew it would shatter me. When I reached Dad, he told me Mum had done one of her disappearing acts shortly before my return. I remember going home and sitting on Dad's lap sobbing. I could feel his jaw clench with anger, but he was very good at pretending nothing was wrong.

As the years rolled by, I felt that Mum and I were losing each other. Our relationship grew more and more distant, and I realised I couldn't believe her lies. I couldn't rely on her or trust her. Still, I always let her know I loved her and needed her to be my mum.

'You've got to stop drinking,' I pleaded over and over again. 'I need you.'

During my teenage years I picked up some bad habits that make me feel ashamed now. 'Fine, you want to drink?' I'd scream in Mum's face. 'Drink, drink, drink. I've got money. Do you want to buy alcohol?'

Afterwards I felt guilt-ridden about my outburst. Years and years of hurt and disappointment had welled up inside me and instead of loving Mum unconditionally, I had boiled over in frustration that I couldn't save her. It is difficult to respect someone who doesn't respect themselves, who doesn't respect you or see the harm they are causing you.

From an early age, Dad instructed me to keep Mum's illness a secret. I hate lying and I feel betrayed when people lie to me, but I wasn't allowed to mention Mum's drinking to anyone, even our closest relatives. It was a taboo topic in our household and difficult to keep secret, but it is how

I learned to put on a front, reminding me of Nat King Cole's song *Smile*.

Smile though your heart is aching
Smile even though it's breaking
When there are clouds in the sky, you'll get by
If you smile through your fear and sorrow
Smile and maybe tomorrow
You'll see the sun come shining through for you.

Smile is the story of my life. As a child I used humour as a deflection, and I still rely on it at times when all hope seems lost. Growing up, some people thought I was silly. They said I didn't take life seriously. In some ways, they were right because the life I was keeping from them was more than serious enough. They didn't know that because I never told them.

One day after returning to boarding school from a trip home, I sat talking to my best friend. I don't know how it happened, but I told her about Mum. It poured out of me and while you'd think I'd have felt relief; I didn't. I felt guilty for going against Dad's instructions. Shame about lacking the picture-perfect, wholesome family of my peers enveloped me. So did the fact that my mother let me down time and again. Would my friend still like me? Would she tell the other girls? Fourteen-year-old girls can be nasty to each other, and I sat in a cold sweat wishing I could take back my words.

My friend was very supportive, but for the first time in my life I had let my protective wall down. Someone now knew my secret and it made me feel vulnerable. I had exposed myself and could no longer pretend I was a happy-go-lucky kid. Instead, I was filled with sadness and heartache that there seemed to be nothing I could do to save my mother from destroying herself and our family.

After confessing the realities of my life home to my friend, I didn't tell anyone else for a few more years. Instead, I hid my tears and acted as the class clown.

Mum, please come home

Mum, Dad and I left Africa and moved to England when I was nearly 17. At first, we lived in a bedsit. It was dingy, but Dad was studying for a master's degree and didn't want to spend too much on rent. He was also planning to buy a house for us once he and Mum found one. I continued at my boarding school until the end of June, then returned to Birmingham for the summer holidays. In September, my parents bought a house, and I started a school closer to home as a weekly boarder. I brimmed with hope that our new life in England would make Mum so happy she would stop drinking.

Shortly after moving into the house, Dad secured a job working in the Falkland Islands. A few days after he left, he phoned me at boarding school. It was unusual for him to call me at school and my throat tightened. I could feel my heart pounding against my chest wall.

'I've had a phone call from the neighbours,' he said in an agitated voice, 'because the kittens cried all day yesterday and right through the night. They're still crying now.'

I left school, returning home to find an empty house.

All too soon, I realised Mum had done another runner. She had left our two little kittens alone and hungry. We didn't know where Mum was or if she was safe. November passed in a blur, then December. I hoped Mum would return home for Christmas, but we didn't hear from her until late January when she telephoned us.

'Please come home, Mum,' I begged, as tears streamed down my cheeks. 'We love you and want you home with us.'

'I can't,' she whimpered. 'I can't. I'm so cold.'

In early March I woke up crying in the middle of the night after dreaming about Mum. It took forever to get back to sleep and for the rest of the night I tossed and turned. When I woke up the next morning, I heard hushed voices in the hallway. I stumbled down the hallway to find a police officer talking to Dad.

'Mum has passed away,' Dad said, reaching out to hug me. His face was ashen, and his eyes brimmed with tears.

I blamed myself for Mum's alcoholism and death. I had tried so hard to rescue her, but my love wasn't enough to save her from her demons. The shock of Mum's passing was so devastating that my body broke out in painful itchy blisters. The doctor said it was shingles. I wasn't allowed to go to Mum's funeral, which rocked me to my core because I couldn't say goodbye to her.

After Mum left me for that last time, I promised myself I would leave no-one. I knew what it was like to be the one left behind and never wanted to inflict that pain on anyone. At the time I didn't know how this decision would later torment me.

My next chapter

During my 30s I lived in New Zealand as a demand planner, allocating stock to my employer's warehouses. My first marriage had ended, but I enjoyed my own company and had a terrific group of friends. I was happy with my life.

My ex-husband had been uber-controlling and took charge of all aspects of our lives, including our finances. My wages used to go into a joint bank account, and my ex allowed me NZ $80 to live off each week. Still, we didn't earn much between us, and we had a mortgage, so I accepted it was necessary to live frugally if we were to get ahead.

After the divorce, I vowed to never again let a man control me. I thought I'd much prefer to be on my own than dominated by my partner, especially one like my ex-husband who betrayed me by having an affair.

One day in October 2007, I was flicking through dating profiles when a photograph caught my eye. The guy in the photo had a big, friendly smile that attracted me. He had enormous brown teddy bear eyes, dark brown hair, and bushy eyebrows. His face looked honest and kind, so I read his profile.

'I just want someone to love me for me, to want me for me,' he wrote, sending shivers up my spine.

My heart skipped a beat. I thought that's exactly what I want. Like most people, I longed for someone to love me for me. Excited but also nervous, I emailed him. To my surprise, he responded in an instant and told me his name was Tom. During the next few days, we emailed back and forth, and the tone gradually became cheekier and more flirtatious.

Tom asked if he could telephone me.

'Yes, of course,' I wrote, holding my breath.

My mobile phone rang a few seconds later. It was Tom. As soon as we started talking, I noticed we shared a similar sense of humour. We hit it off straight away, joking about the Muppets and incidents from our childhood we'd found funny. Quickly, the conversation turned to how badly Tom felt he'd been treated by his family. Growing up, Tom believed his parents had favoured his brother and sister and that he always came off second best. No matter what he did to please his parents, nothing worked, leaving him feel bereft, heartbroken and distressed. It surprised me that Tom confided his innermost feelings with me so soon after we made contact.

Tom said he'd been married and divorced twice and that he'd tried to commit suicide earlier that year by overdose. Fortunately, his boss broke into his house and managed to get him to the hospital in time and saved his life. Like me, Tom's greatest dream was to start a family and his disastrous marriages left him feeling like it would never happen. Tom told me he worked in the film editing business and that he also had a job as a service manager at a car dealership. During the conversation, he talked about his BMW and the string of investment properties he and his ex-wife owned. He also regaled me with details of his palatial Adelaide home in a compound next-door to the tennis champion Lleyton Hewitt. I knew Lleyton Hewitt had been born in Adelaide, but I thought he and his wife

Bec lived in Melbourne. I let it go, thinking maybe I was wrong. Anyway, I reassured myself, in the scheme of things, it really wasn't important. I was so wrong to dismiss it, but I didn't realise my mistake until it was too late.

During that first phone call, my heart was on fire, and I felt an instant connection with Tom. He said he felt the same about me. It's difficult to describe that sense of us being kindred spirits. It was almost immediate and had never happened to me before. Tom told me he was searching for a life partner. He didn't want to waste his time on frivolous relationships and wanted a lifetime commitment. Like me, he yearned to have children, and he shared his dream of building a family with his soulmate. We both agreed the foundations of a good relationship were trust and honesty and that we wouldn't settle for anything less than this. To my surprise, he ticked all my boxes!

'All I want is someone who's honest, loving, kind, supportive and trustworthy,' I said. Little did I know how he would later use this comment against me.

As we said 'goodbye', my head swooned. I glanced at my watch and realised three hours had passed. My head and heart were alive with the possibilities that lay ahead.

The following day, my phone rang before dawn. I was in a deep sleep, but my eyes flew open, thinking the alarm clock had gone off. But it was still pitch-black outside. Still in a dreamy state, I answered. It was Tom. We chatted for ages while I luxuriated in the warmth of my bedclothes. When it was time to shower, I told him I had to go.

'Do you have to go already,' he whined, making me feel guilty.

'Yes, I must get ready for work.'

I jumped in the shower. A couple of minutes later, I heard my phone ringing. I thought I'd leave it, but it kept ringing, so I answered it in case it was Dad or my boss. Dripping wet, I answered it, leaving puddles on the bathroom floor and hallway. To my surprise, it was Tom. We talked while I dressed, put on my makeup, styled my hair and tried to eat a bowl of muesli without crunching too noisily in his ear. My heart raced with the excitement of Tom's fervour, but also with the panic of arriving late for my first meeting of the day. We said our goodbyes, and I floated to work on cloud nine. As soon as I arrived at my desk, my phone rang. It was Tom. I tried to explain that I was due at a meeting and couldn't talk for long, but he sounded crestfallen.

That day passed with my head in a haze, then as soon as I arrived home, my mobile phone rang. It was Tom. We chatted while I cooked dinner and got ready for bed, a pattern that continued every day for months. Love letters flew back and forth between us, but some of them surprised me because of the way Tom confided in me. What he confessed were secrets I thought couples shared after they'd been together for many years. Through his confidences, Tom made me feel we were meant to be together. He moved the relationship forward very quickly. It surprised me, but I went along with it because he made me feel we'd found each other. At last, we'd each met our soulmate. Our budding relationship was built on a simpatico I had never previously experienced. Deep down I felt flattered that he found me so interesting he wanted to speak with me so often.

Tom made me feel loved and secure by truly listening to me and showering me with compliments. Saying I was beautiful and kind, he kept calling me 'amazing'. Vowing to always love me, he promised he'd never be controlling like my ex or do anything to harm me. Something I noticed early on was how polite Tom was towards me. In our phone calls and emails, he never swore, so whenever I was on the verge of swearing, I hesitated, thinking I'd better not do it in case it put him off me.

A few weeks after we started emailing each other, Tom told me he was about to lose a $15 million investment in a production company in Australia.

'The board members are meeting now,' he said. 'I'll know later today if I'm to lose everything.'

'Well, I know you as you are without it, so it doesn't bother me,' I said. A person's wealth doesn't interest me, and I didn't know what it would be like to have or lose $15 million. It was irrelevant to me.

The next day, Tom telephoned. 'I've lost everything,' he sighed.

I tried to reassure him that it didn't affect the way I felt about him, and I liked him for himself, with or without money.

Frequent phone calls from Tom continued, but it got to the point that I struggled to find topics to talk about. Feverish phone calls are understandable for the first couple of weeks when you're excited about a new relationship, and you want to ask each other about everything. But months down the track? And I felt many of the conversations were too heavy, especially when Tom spoke about his childhood.

In early December 2007, he flew across to New Zealand to meet me. When I met him at the airport, my heart sank. He wore scruffy denim shorts and a faded Wallabies' jersey. Although I too dressed casually, it was chic casual, and I had gone to a lot of effort to make myself look attractive.

'I see you dressed up,' I joked, trying to cover my disappointment.

Tom smirked. 'Well, I didn't want to make a big effort and dress up just in case you didn't turn up or what we had felt on the phone wasn't there.'

I felt a knot in the pit of my stomach tighten.

After getting over the anticlimax of Tom's shabby clothes, I noticed his huge hands. They looked strong, as did his arm muscles that were pumped from working out at the gym. Quite stocky, his protruding barrel stomach made him look like a cuddly teddy bear. I liked his looks, but Tom didn't seem as confident in person as he had appeared on the phone. Surprisingly, I didn't feel the same level of connection with him. I tried to push aside these thoughts but being ever hopeful of meeting my match, I dismissed them.

Once we had a couple of glasses of wine, Tom seemed to relax and exude the same confidence and charisma I remembered from our phone calls. That first night we enjoyed a romantic dinner at one of my favourite Auckland restaurants. During the meal, Tom promised to always protect me. He had a solicitous air about him, making me feel he would look after me forever.

The next day we hung out in Auckland and revelled in each other's company. We shared many laughs and got along well. During the afternoon we played pool, and Tom beat me. It was obvious he was extremely competitive, so much so that it put me off playing any sort of game with him because I play to have fun rather than to win. That second evening we went to a Thai restaurant. The food was delicious, and I relished the vibe between Tom and me. Maybe we are meant for each other I thought to myself?

Midway through the meal, Tom became agitated and seemed to choke. Struggling to breathe, he looked ill. We left the restaurant early, returning home, where Tom collapsed into bed and fell asleep instantly. And that's where he stayed for the rest of the night, sleeping off an MSG reaction.

The following day, Tom was due to fly back to Australia. He got up silently, packed, then waited for me to dress and find my car keys. It felt like an odd way to end our time together. Sad to see Tom leave me after such a short visit, I drove him to Auckland Airport. During the trip I struggled to hold back my tears. On the escalator, Tom turned towards me, smiled his most gorgeous smile and gave me a big, goofy wave. As I turned to leave the terminal, I had never felt more alone.

Despite the low points, Tom's visit cemented our relationship. Soon after he returned home, he invited me to spend Christmas with him and his family. I was ecstatic and booked tickets for the flight to Australia.

When I arrived at Tom's family home on Christmas Eve, his parents and sister warmly welcomed me. They made me feel secure, happy and excited about the future.

On Christmas afternoon while we sat around chatting after savouring roast turkey and plum pudding, the phone rang. Tom's sister answered it. She called out to Tom that it was his ex-wife.

It seemed strange that Tom's ex would call when she knew his new partner was present. On Christmas evening, once we were alone, I asked Tom about it.

'Look,' he smiled reassuringly, 'I told her I was going to be here and that you'd be here with me.'

The festive spirit of the day evaporated in an instant, and my jaw clenched. 'Why is she phoning you if the marriage is over and she knows you have a new partner?' I asked. 'I have no contact with my ex-husband.'

Tom hugged me. 'Just trust me, please trust me.'

After Christmas I returned to New Zealand. The trip left me with a few lingering doubts about Tom, but I tried to brush them away because I felt attracted to him and he ticked so many of my boxes.

Tom flew to New Zealand for New Year's Eve celebrations at a pub with some of my closest friends. During the party, he kept popping in and out of the bar to talk on the phone.

'It's strange the way he keeps going out to make phone calls,' my friend said, frowning.

The next day, I asked Tom about the phone calls.

'Ah, I was phoning my friends to tell them how much of a great time I was having with you. I wanted to wish them 'Happy New Year'.

Later that day after sharing brunch with my friends, Tom dropped a bombshell.

'I'm not divorced,' he admitted sheepishly. 'We're separated.'

His admission took my breath away.

'I told you honesty and truth were important to me,' I said, trying to keep my voice calm and steady. 'We agreed we would base our relationship on being truly open with each other. I've been honest with you about everything.'

He shrugged, glancing away.

Tom returned to Australia, and his pattern of repeated phone calls at each hour of the day and night, continued. In one conversation, he contradicted himself, making a claim that was 360 degrees from what he told me the previous week. I had noticed him doing it before but never thought to question him.

'But you told me a different version of that story last week,' I said, confused about what he'd told me.

His voice took on an aggressive tone and he started to bully me verbally. He obviously didn't like me calling him out.

In April 2008, Tom's sister phoned me. We chatted happily, and I felt we were getting to know each other. At one point in the conversation, she paused.

'I just hope Tom stops his bullshit,' she said. My stomach sank. She explained that she and her younger brother were sick of the way Tom viewed everybody else as the problem and not himself. I didn't know how to react. I'd already noticed this issue but tried to dismiss it.

During the following months, I noticed Tom often contradicted himself or told me stories about his past that didn't add up. At times, what he told me made little sense. I'm an analytical person and whenever something doesn't make sense, I feel uncomfortable. I feel that something is wrong and try to work it out. Whenever Tom's stories didn't feel right, I questioned him. But he became defensive and tried to talk his way out of it. He put me into a corner, where I either had to accept his explanation or not. And if I didn't accept it, he would tell me to 'fuck off'.

In 2008, my employer held a staff retreat in Queenstown. Tom flew from Melbourne to be with me. Even though he knew I shared a hotel room with a colleague, Tom rang me at five o'clock in the morning. I felt intensely fatigued, my throat was on fire and my nose dripped constantly. When I answered the phone in an unusually deep husky voice, I started sneezing.

'Oh, so you're not well, and I've flown all this way,' he whined. 'I'm the one who is tired.'

Tom and I had booked a hotel room in Queenstown, and I moved across to stay with him. But he was obnoxious, making me feel like I had ruined his fantasy of what the four days were going to be like. Even at that early stage I could see Tom had mental battles, and there was a lot going on in his head. Something about him made me feel uneasy, but I couldn't put my figure on it. I think he sensed my agitation and went all out to make me love him.

During the visit Tom alternated between punishing me for being unwell then acting as if he was the kindest person in the world. It was terribly confusing. He made me feel he was the positive person, and I was the negative one. To a certain degree, he was positive, but it could go from one extreme to another in the blink of an eye. He'd say nice things to me and about me, then the next minute he would call me every filthy name under the sun. It did my head in. I wondered how someone who says he loves you could talk like that and be like that? It took little effort on his part to get inside my head and wreak havoc. That's the scary part. I wish a friend had told me to end the relationship, but I didn't open up and tell anyone what was happening. Now I ask myself, 'Why didn't I leave him?'

Tom made me feel like I was crazy and reading too much into what he told me. Time and again I tried to push away my unease because it didn't fit with my fantasy about Tom as my perfect partner. Also, I try to see the best in people, and I kept making excuses for him. The more I noticed his contradictions, the more my anxiety went through the roof. I desperately wanted our relationship to work. I truly believed I could help Tom with his emotional issues, and we could create our happy ending.

Starting over

One year after meeting Tom, I moved to Australia to live with him. It was an enormous step to take but I felt good about it. Within a week of arriving, Tom said my money was 'his money' or 'our money'. I felt uncomfortable and a creeping sense of dread enveloped me because it reminded me of my ex-husband. 'No, no, no, no, no, no, no, no,' I screamed inside. But on the outside, I smiled, deep down dismissing the red flags.

A few months later, I had intense abdominal pain and bleeding. To my dismay, I discovered I had two ovarian cysts that had erupted. I needed an operation, urgently. Afterwards, my surgeon took me aside.

'If you want to get pregnant, you need to get pregnant now to stop these cysts coming back,' he advised.

Tom and I longed to have children, but despite our best efforts, I couldn't fall pregnant. During this time, Tom often shouted at me or put me down. He continually second-guessed me and hurled abuse at me. Increasingly, he took control over our finances, where we went, who we saw and what we ate. His accusations and the disgusting names he called me cut deep. No-one had ever spoken to me that way. It is hard to feel desire for someone who is so vindictive towards you. Sometimes he even mentioned my mother, claiming: 'It's your fault she was an alcoholic, you drove her to drink.'

You might well ask why I stayed. Why did I try to get pregnant with Tom when our relationship was faltering? The answer is that it's complex, a weak excuse I now know. There were things I loved about Tom and our relationship. He showered me with compliments, especially on Facebook. Saying how much he thought of me, he built up an image of an adoring partner. He portrayed himself as the good guy. And at times he could be a good guy. Tom was hysterically funny, and we shared many belly laughs together. When we first met, we used to laugh and joke about what our kids would be like. I yearned to start a family. At 37, I knew the chances of me meeting someone who would father my children were minimal.

During 2009, we continued our attempts to get pregnant, and I had three rounds of artificial insemination. But it didn't work. The following year I had two rounds of IVF, but I found the need to have sex on certain days and the IVF drugs killed my sex drive. I didn't feel sexy anymore and blamed it on the IVF because it took the fun out of our sex life. Making love became functional, almost a chore.

The hormones I took with each round of IVF messed with my moods, and I became hypersensitive to Tom's toxic insults. My inability to conceive made me feel guilty and ashamed, and I felt I was disappointing Tom. I thought maybe that was why his behaviour towards me was so vindictive. With each passing week, our fights escalated, and I stopped feeling attracted to Tom. How can you expect to desire someone who denigrates you? I kept apologising to him about my lack of desire, but each time I did, a venomous response gushed from his mouth. I couldn't believe my partner and the man I was planning to be the father of my children would speak to me that way.

After the second round of IVF, I was delighted to discover I was pregnant. The doctor phoned me at work to tell me. Before I fell pregnant, whenever Tom and I talked about how it would make us feel, he said, 'I'll be so excited, I'll be telling everyone.'

I couldn't wait to share the news with Tom, so dropped what I was doing at work and drove to his car dealership. I was excited and emotional, thinking I was about to give him the best news ever. Maybe it would be what we needed to mend our tattered relationship? When I arrived, I jumped from my car and raced into the dealership.

Out of breath, I spotted Tom in the workshop. He was servicing a blue Mazda. 'I'm pregnant,' I gasped.

'Oh, that's great,' he said in a flat voice before turning his back to me and resuming his servicing.

'I thought you'd be happier than this,' I said, tears welling up in my eyes.

'So, I'm at fault because I'm not acting the way you wanted me to react?'

I didn't want him to respond in any particular way, but I assumed he would be more excited than he appeared, especially after all our conversations about how we thought we would behave.

During my pregnancy, Tom and I often argued and when I was seven months pregnant, he pushed me into a chest of drawers. The right side of my chest hit the sharp edge of the cabinet. The force of impact was so strong that ornaments sitting on top fell on the floor and smashed. I was heartbroken because I'd given the ornaments to my nan when I was a child, and after her death, my relatives returned them to me as a keepsake.

My ribs turned black and blue, and I worried the fall might have hurt my unborn baby. But Tom played it down. 'Oh, for God's sake, it was just a gentle push,' he sneered.

I didn't tell anyone about the attack or even check in with my GP. WHY NOT? I now ask myself.

Our beautiful son Daniel was born nine months later and much to my relief, he was healthy. When he was a couple of weeks old, Tom and I had an argument. Daniel was asleep in his cot, and Tom threatened to take him away from me because he claimed I was a hopeless mother. Tom bent forward over Daniel's cot, to pick him up. I tried to stop him, but he pushed me so violently I stumbled and fell. I fought back to protect my son.

I felt intensely protective of Daniel and worried that Tom might hurt him during one of his outbursts of temper. Tom sensed my caution and ranted about it. To keep the peace, I just had to let it go. Still, Tom could be a good father, happily changing Daniel's nappy, feeding him and keeping him entertained. This relieved my anxiety to some extent, but I also had a nagging doubt in the back of my mind.

When Daniel was three months old, we flew to Western Australia because Tom had been invited to a job interview there. In the hotel room after the interview, Tom said something to me. I responded, then he muttered a derogatory comment under his breath.

'What?' I asked, jiggling Daniel up and down gently to soothe him.

'You're unstable,' Tom hissed. 'I'm taking Daniel away from you. I'm reporting you to the department as a bad mother.'

Tom yelled in my face, and Daniel started crying. The more Tom roared, the more Daniel screamed, further infuriating Tom, who bellowed even louder.

The next day when we arrived home, we had another argument. I tried to rest on my bed, but Tom followed me, spewing a tirade of abuse. He jumped onto the bed, shaking his fist in the air. I was afraid he was going to hit me.

Tom was offered the job in Western Australia, so we moved there. I thought it would be a terrific opportunity for us to make a new start. But the arguments and verbal abuse continued as before, dashing my hopes of a reconciliation.

When Daniel was six months old, I was due for an embryo transfer. I didn't want to bring another baby into such an abusive relationship, so told Tom I wasn't going through with the transfer. But he raged at me. I tried to stand up for myself, which led to another vicious argument. In the end, he cajoled me into it.

To my surprise and delight, I fell pregnant on my first round of treatment. But it was a difficult pregnancy, and I often spotted. It made me edgy, and arguments with Tom were a constant. I called my best friend in the United Kingdom because I feared for my life and that of my unborn baby. But I was trapped in a new country and knew no-one except Tom's family and friends.

When I was 25 weeks pregnant, we flew to the UK. Before we left, Tom admitted there were problems at his car dealership. At the time I visited him at work, and he looked out of his depth even though he'd been in similar roles for more than five years. He said he was having trouble with management, something to do with the way they wanted to manage their price points. Tom accused them of illegal practices.

'I can't work with a business that does that,' he said.

Despite the uncertainty of Tom's position, we flew to England. One night, we had an argument in the cottage we rented. Daniel was asleep and as I went to walk down the stairs away from Tom, he grabbed my hair, pulling me backwards. I almost lost my footing and fell down the rest of the stairwell. There was also an upset on the way back to Australia at Heathrow when the security officer told us to empty Daniel's bottles of milk. Tom raged at him, and I worried he would be arrested for his aggression.

While we waited in the plane to taxi onto the runway, I wished I had the strength to remain in England, rather than returning home with an abusive partner. Again, why didn't I?

Within a week of us returning to Australia, Tom phoned me from work.

'Look, I've had a meeting with management. They've said that either I do it their way or I leave. I can't ethically do it the way they want me to do it.'

I gritted my teeth, worrying about how we would pay our bills, but I said: 'Leave. It's your only option. We'll work it out.'

Shortly afterwards, Tom got a job as a service adviser, but it wasn't as senior, so he earned less than before.

Tom's abuse put me on edge all the time because I never knew when he would explode. I tried to mollify him. It was like walking on eggshells, and I was apprehensive all the time, worried I might trigger his temper. He seemed to thrive on making me doubt myself, my memories and judgement. The low self-esteem I had brought into our relationship from my childhood increased and strangely, this made me more dependent on Tom for emotional support and validation. The way he contradicted me every time I said something undermined me so much that I totally lost my confidence and sense of self-worth.

Why didn't I tell anyone about Tom's abuse? I think he had convinced me I was the problem. Tom seemed to be the confident, happy one who was the most secure out of the two of us. Whereas for me, I felt like I was the worrier. I wasn't as confident as him. Tom seemed to know everyone and was known as 'Fun Tommy', Tommy who would do anything for anyone at any time of the day or night. He'd drop whatever he was doing and help a mate or his parents. It put me at a disadvantage because I was the newbie on his patch. I didn't think anyone would have believed me because they couldn't imagine Tom would do what he did to me.

'What, Tommy?' I thought his family and friends would say. 'Tommy? No way. He wouldn't do that. He loves you.'

I talked to a couple of people about the arguments, but I didn't reveal the psychological and physical abuse. No-one would have believed me because Tom was so jolly around his family and friends. He came across a kind, caring person. Whenever we watched the news and it showed stories of abusive relationships, Tom appeared genuinely horrified that someone would hurt their partner. It didn't seem like he was pretending to be horrified, as if he didn't realise he was abusive and cruel towards me. I now regret that I didn't open up and tell anyone what was happening.

An anxious time

One day six weeks before my baby was due, I started bleeding, but I had frequent episodes of bleeding throughout my pregnancy so tried to remain calm. My unborn baby was moving around and kicking, so I thought she was okay. The next morning, I felt intensely hormonal and emotional. Tom was at work and his mum was staying with us, so she looked after Daniel while I drove to see my GP. Tom met me there. The GP sent me straight to hospital, and the obstetrician hooked me up to the fetal heart rate monitor and other devices. He said I was fine, and the baby's heartbeat was normal.

The doctor and nurses left us because everything seemed to be okay, but I suddenly felt a weird sensation all over my body. In the same instant, my baby's heart rate changed, and I felt a sharp stabbing pain on my side. The obstetrician and nurses ran into my room.

'Right, you're having your baby now,' they said calmly although I sensed they were trying to hide their panic. 'Your placenta's bursting so we're going to get you into theatre as quickly as possible.'

From then on, everything seemed to happen in slow

motion. I was disappointed to not be able to give birth naturally but was ecstatic when I discovered my baby was a girl, as I had hoped. We named her Sophie.

Two days later, I visited Sophie in the nursery. The paediatrician and nurse were standing by her crib. When they spotted me, they fell silent. The paediatrician was scowling, and the nurse evaded eye contact with me. I sensed something was wrong and edged closer to the crib.

'Look, I'm sorry,' the paediatrician said, 'but we're going to have to test Sophie for Down syndrome.'

The following hours unfolded at a snail's pace while we waited for the test results. I desperately needed reassurance from Tom, but he wasn't an overly affectionate person. He would sometimes hug, but it was never the deep, nurturing, caring cuddle I craved.

Finally, two days later, the results of Sophie's test arrived. Much to our relief, she didn't have Down syndrome. But she had to remain in neonatal intensive care because she wasn't putting on weight and had complications with her bowels from the milk formula.

I remained in hospital with Sophie, and Tom looked after Daniel at home. But Tom always made me feel like he was the worst one off, having a harder time looking after Daniel and doing all the household chores on his own. He claimed that I had it easy sitting all day in the hospital room with Sophie. We had many arguments in that room. Everyone including new parents and the nurses would have heard; it was so embarrassing.

Four weeks later when Sophie came home from hospital, I noticed Tom didn't bond with her. It worried me and I wondered how I could encourage him to connect with his beautiful baby daughter.

One day soon after arriving home, Tom and I were in the living room together. Tom was holding Sophie. He was shouting at me, then threw his ham and tomato sandwich in my face. To my horror, he held Sophie over the couch and looked as if he would let her fall onto it. I screamed at him to leave her alone. In desperation I called the police.

The police ended up removing Tom from home for a few days.

After a fight, instead of apologising, Tom would blame me for what had happened. He said it was my fault, and I had provoked him. When I called the police, his reaction floored me.

'I can't believe you've phoned the police,' he would hiss.

He made me feel everything was my fault, and he was the victim. I'd pushed him to hit me. It was my fault he was in trouble with the police.

After one argument, Tom took a knife into the bathroom, ran a bath, then sat in it saying there was no point in living.

'If you really want to do it, go somewhere else,' I said calmly. 'I don't want Daniel to see.' I didn't care anymore. Tom was attention seeking, and I wasn't buying it.

Still, I worried about Tom's mental health and encouraged him to see a doctor and counsellor. But he refused.

On New Year's Eve, when Sophie was seven months old, she developed a fever and her face looked puffy. We took her to emergency and after several tests discovered she had inherited spherocytosis, a condition in which the red blood cells are an oval shape. Tom had spherocytosis, and so did his mother. From then on Sophie had weekly blood tests and regular check-ups. We also gave her folic acid every day. It was a worrying time.

Tom and I continued to argue, and in one fight when Sophie was 12 months old, I fled to the ensuite next to our bedroom. Tom followed me, then lurched and grabbed my throat. He pushed me up against the wall. With his enormous fist, he bashed my face. It scared the shit out of me. I sent photos of the bruises to a friend who was an ex-British cop in Western Australia, but I didn't report Tom to the police. Why not, you might ask? I ask myself the same question every day. I should have left, but I longed for my kids to grow up in a happy family with a mother and father, so I stayed. Given what unfolded, I now regret that decision.

I suppose in some ways I felt like I deserved Tom's abuse. His excuse was that I didn't give him enough love, I didn't do enough for him. I didn't do this. I didn't do that. He made me feel guilty. Maybe he was right because I was consumed by the needs of our two small babies. During some disputes Tom would say: 'I do so much for you. I come home and play with Daniel, and I help you around the house.' He was a good father, and I knew from many other mums that their partners didn't spend time with their kids or pitch in with the chores. And here I was. I had someone who was a devoted father.

In August 2013 when Sophie was 16 months old, she was diagnosed with hip dysplasia. Her right hip joint was dislocated, so she was fitted with a half body cast from the waist to the toes for three months. From about 10 months, I had noticed that she couldn't put weight on her right leg when most babies can stand with assistance at that age. But I tried not to worry because every child attains their milestones differently and I didn't want to be seen as neurotic.

To our great surprise, Tom was offered a service manager position on the south coast of New South Wales. We moved there in May 2014. Soon after, Sophie took her first steps, a delightful surprise after the cumbersome brace she had to wear.

Disappointingly, things were not looking good on-the-job front. The manager at Tom's car dealership bullied him mercilessly. I felt sorry for him because he was so badly targeted. In desperation, Tom applied for a role as a service manager in regional Victoria.

Fortunately, Tom got the job in Victoria, so we moved there in 2015. He did well in this job, and I finally felt as if I could breathe again. Still, given his history of issues at work I was always on edge worrying about what might go wrong.

No! It can't be true

In April 2015, my stepfather whom I considered as my dad because he had raised me so lovingly since I was six months old, suddenly died. I was devastated, desperately needing cuddles and compassion, but Tom told me to 'get over it' and 'move on'.

Two months later, I noticed that Sophie was lethargic and pale. When the results from her weekly blood test arrived showing her red cell count at 50—it should be a minimum of 110—I panicked. We rushed her to the local hospital for tests and a blood transfusion. Sophie gradually recovered but over the next three months, she needed three more blood transfusions.

In October Sophie ended up at a Children's Hospital in Melbourne. The paediatrician read her test results and scowled. I tried to make eye contact with him, but he avoided my gaze.

'I need to do a lumbar puncture,' he mumbled.

Panic surged through me. I couldn't bear to think of Sophie in pain. 'Will Sophie be sedated?'

The doctor smiled. 'Yes, she'll be asleep. She won't feel a thing.'

After Sophie's lumbar puncture we had a terrifying two-hour wait for the result. I popped downstairs to buy some bottled water and Tom stayed with Sophie and Daniel in the hospital room. Just as the lift reached the ground floor, my mobile phone rang.

'Leena,' Tom said, 'the doctor's here. You need to come back up now.'

When I returned, Tom was in the room with Sophie.

My heart skipped a beat. 'Where's Daniel?'

'A volunteer is looking after him,' Tom whispered.

I thought we must be in for terrible news. At that point, two doctors entered the room.

'We've done a test,' one of them said. His face was ashen, and he had dark circles under his eyes.

'Yes, yes, yes,' I said, 'just tell me what she's got. Please, just tell me what she's got.'

The doctor looked at his feet. 'It's acute lymphoblastic leukaemia.'

My universe collapsed in that moment. Sophie was only three and a half and I couldn't bear to see her suffer. Her chemo started the very next day. The cancer cells had infiltrated Sophie's spinal fluid, so the chemo drugs were injected into her spinal canal to help prevent the leukaemia reaching her brain—once in the brain it is almost impossible to remove the cancer cells, so it was a race against time.

The oncologist implanted a port on Sophie's left side, which the doctors accessed with a needle when they needed to inject large volumes of drugs. The first 28 days were absolutely crucial, and Sophie was pumped full of steroids. She also endured round after round of painful tests. The drugs burned Sophie's colon and she suffered excruciating abdominal pain. Her poo was full of acid and toxic chemicals, and she became constipated because it was too painful to defecate. Several times during the treatment, Sophie would start screaming and shaking.

'My poo, my poo,' she would screech between sobs.

Each time it happened, I would rush her upstairs, put on gloves, lie her on the bed, prop up her legs, then manually pull out the poo. It was excruciatingly painful for both of us. I tried to be gentle, but it didn't help much because Sophie's body was so badly burned from the corrosive drugs.

Whenever Sophie's port had to be accessed to administer chemo, one of us, Tom or me, would lie on the recliner and Sophie would sit on our lap. We would hold down her arms and put both our legs over hers. It was terribly traumatic for Sophie, and I felt helpless to reduce her suffering. Her screams during the procedure were heartrending and are etched in my memory. I'll never forget them.

For eight months we stayed at Ronald McDonald House in Melbourne. I'd stay for a week with Sophie while Tom remained at home with Daniel, then they would visit for the weekend, and we'd swap over. Tom would remain in Melbourne, and I would return to regional Victoria with Daniel.

As you can imagine, this was a deeply emotional time for us all. One day while sobbing I rang Tom.

'This isn't about you,' he hissed. 'This is about Sophie. Pull yourself together.'

Tom and I argued a lot during Sophie's treatment and Tom often became aggressive, so much so that a hospital social worker became involved. However, other times Tom was supportive and loving. We made a deal that whoever was in hospital with Sophie had priority—if they were having a bad day, they could vent their frustrations first. We agreed that whatever was happening at home wasn't as important as the turmoil of being at the hospital. Sometimes we'd be so strong together and then other days we'd descend into bitter conflict.

One day in oncology, I waited for the doctor to see Sophie. She was tired and grumpy. While I sat there hoping for good news, I turned and mumbled something to Tom.

His face turned black, and his eyes blazed with fury. 'Don't you even fuckin' talk to me like that,' he thundered.

Episodes of snapping like that astonished me because Tom would progress from 0 to 100 in an instant. One minute we would be in-sync and laughing together, and the next he would be raging about something I had done or not done, said or not said.

After several outbursts, I thought, 'That's it, I'm done.'

Tom would blame me for his outbursts of hatred. It was always my fault. 'I'm only retaliating,' he snarled. '99.9 percent of the time I'm retaliating.'

I was gobsmacked. 'So what you're saying is, 0.01% of the time it's your fault?'

'Yes, I only ever retaliate, Leena.'

After Sophie was diagnosed with leukaemia, Tom resigned from his job because one of us had to be with Sophie and the other had to be with Daniel, who was only four. We chewed up our superannuation on living and medical expenses, then in desperation borrowed money from our family. But it was not enough to continue paying the rent, and we were within two weeks of becoming homeless. It was terrifying. To feel you've got no money and a critically ill child, I don't know how it didn't break us. I felt so guilty that I'd brought Daniel and Sophie into this world, and all they'd experienced was pain and heartache. You don't bring children into the world for that.

During Sophie's treatment, when I was at my most vulnerable, Tom targeted me at the core of my being, making me further question my sense of identity and self-worth. His lies and the misinformation he fed me made me question things I knew were true. Was I too gullible? Or did I want to believe? I ended up doubting my memory, judgements and even my sanity.

In hindsight, Tom was manipulating me to gain the upper hand. He wanted complete power over me. Sometimes he showered me with compliments but behind my back Tom tried to turn my friends and his family against me by claiming I was lying or delusional. Several times during Sophie's treatment I had no other option than to take out an intervention order because he attacked me. He would grab me by the throat then bash my face so brutally I ended up with enormous black eyes.

One day when Sophie was in the maintenance stage of

treatment and home for a few days, Tom was downstairs in the garage.

'Are you okay to pick up Daniel, Tom?' I sang out from the living room.

He exploded, accusing me of ordering him to drive Daniel home. Afterwards, Tom and I sat together on the deck smoking a cigarette.

'What's going on, Tom?' I said, I just called out to you and asked whether you minded collecting Daniel.'

'No, you didn't Leena, no you didn't say that.'

'I did, Tom. I know what I said. I just don't get what's going on.'

I tried to placate him, but the more I tried the more aggressive and abusive he became.

'Oh, for fuck's sake, Tom,' I blurted out without thinking.

In that instant, Tom pushed back his chair noisily, stood up, then punched me in the eye. The force of impact was so strong my chair tumbled over the side of the deck. Tom jumped to the ground and started kicking me viciously. I screamed and our next-door neighbours heard us.

'Leena, are you okay?' they yelled. 'Leena, are you all right?

'Help, help, help,' I screamed.

Daniel, Sophie and I escaped to our neighbour's home, where I called the police. That time, Tom was charged, and we went to court. Before the hearing Tom looked at me pleadingly.

'If you don't drop the charges, Leena, we'll never be able to go to England to see your family,' he insisted.

At the hearing I looked up at the judge. 'I want to drop the charges,' I said, my insides curdling.

The judge ordered Tom to attend an anger management course and counselling. Every time Tom returned from the anger management sessions, he would tell me about the stories he heard from other abusive men. He was astonished they could be so violent towards their partners and children.

The anger management and counselling made no difference to Tom's behaviour towards me. He knew how to manipulate everyone around him and put on a good show. His counsellor mediated us a couple of times and he corrected Tom when he misunderstood or misrepresented what I said. During one mediation session while Tom was in the bathroom, I asked the counsellor if Tom would change.

'It's very unlikely,' he sighed. 'He doesn't recognise he has any issues and believes he is blameless.'

The worst thing about being abused is feeling you're the only one and you're alone. And Tom played on this. Right from the get-go, and every time we had an argument, he threatened to leave me. He knew it was my weak point. Why didn't I leave? What was I afraid of that would happen to me? Is it because I know what it's like to be left? I don't want anyone else feeling like that. Why do I not have the energy to walk away from someone who is not good for me? In Tom's case, was it because he promised me children? That was the bargaining chip.

Surprisingly, Tom accused me of using him to have children. That floored me because from our first conversation we shared our dream of starting a family. I believed in our dream, but I think there were aspects of Tom's dream that I wasn't fulfilling to his satisfaction.

If you accept...
Do you forgive?

People saw the good Tom, the happy Tom, the fun Tom, the kind Tom. They didn't always see Tom's other side. I couldn't talk to anyone about my problems because I didn't think they'd believe me. Tom told everyone I was crazy, and he said his family and friends didn't like me. He isolated me. Still, we did have fun times, especially with Daniel and Sophie. One night when we sat at the dining table chatting after dinner, Sophie was annoying Tom with her antics.

'Sophie, pack it in,' he said. 'I don't want to hear another peep out of you.'

Sophie gave her dad her prettiest smile. 'Peep,' she giggled.

It was hysterical, but Tom and I tried not to laugh. Moments like this were the ones I treasured most. They kept me hoping Tom's behaviour might change.

We were overjoyed when Sophie finished chemo on New Year's Eve in 2017. She's been in remission ever since and growing stronger each day. She asks: 'Why me?' but I don't have an adequate answer for her. I feel guilty about it and wish I could say something that would make her feel better about her ordeal. Her bravery through it astonished me and made me feel intensely proud of her.

Once Sophie was in remission, Tom kept promising he would get a job. 'I'm going to go back into filming and editing,' he said. But he didn't bring in any money and I was getting desperate about our financial situation. In 2018, I noticed an advertisement in the local newspaper that caught my eye. Someone needed a cleaner to do an end of lease clean.

'I'm going to do it,' I said, excited at the prospect of earning some money. 'I'll set up a cleaning business.'

'I'll do it with you,' Tom said.

But Tom quickly took over control of the business, dictating how I should manage it. If I didn't obey his instructions, he would become angry and he constantly accused me of doing things incorrectly. The more I questioned some of his business decisions, the angrier he would get. He would twist things around, deflect what I said and throw issues back onto me. I kept suggesting ways we could increase our income, but he would say: 'You don't get rich in business. You have a better lifestyle.'

Tom would often interrupt me whenever I spoke with my staff, and he was around. He would undermine me in front them and warn me to be less friendly with them. 'You're getting too close,' he'd say. But at times he encouraged and supported me, all the while controlling every aspect of the business. It was terribly confusing.

Tom refused to listen to me. When we disagreed, the issue was always resolved on his terms. If our conversation became heated and I didn't agree with him, he would tell me the relationship was over, that it wasn't working anymore. Often, I walked away to avoid a quarrel, but Tom would follow me, cursing me, shouting, putting me down. He wouldn't leave me alone and rang me constantly when we were apart.

Often when we spoke about an argument once everything was calm, I'd lose the conversation.

'Can we just sit down and talk?' I'd say, trying to stay calm.

Tom would blame the conflict on the way I treated him, how I'd done him wrong, and how he was the victim.

'Tom, would you please listen to me?' I would plead. 'Please listen to what I'm trying to say. I'm not angry, but I just need you to listen to me.'

'Okay. Go on, go on.'

He'd listen for a while then interrupt, shouting at the top of his voice.

'Please let me finish?' I'd say. 'You've said your piece. It's my turn now.'

All too soon, I would notice Tom's jaw clench, a sign his temper was about to flare.

On the other hand, some days everything would be terrific, and we would get along well. We had fun together sharing laughs and hanging out with Daniel and Sophie doing normal family things like picnics and trips to the beach. Those were my happiest days. They made up for the bad times and kept me in the relationship.

Is accepting a person's abusive behaviour towards you a form of forgiveness? Do you accept because you realise that is who they are, and they won't change? In yielding, do you forsake your own morals, values and beliefs? Does this show the other person you forgive them? If so, is this a sign of strength or weakness on your part? Staying takes strength. Leaving takes strength. Is forgiving a cop-out by excusing them for their hurtful words and actions, so that you don't have to make the choice to leave or stay?

Fantasy versus reality

Often during Victoria's long COVID-19 lockdowns Tom and I grated against each other. There was no escape from the constant conflict. Lockdowns are challenging for everyone, but they are disastrous when one partner in a relationship is abusive because there is no way of releasing the pressure from minor irritations and disagreements. The tension builds up then a tiny issue blown out of all proportion can cause it to escalate. That was what life was like for us for throughout 2020. The lockdowns were also stressful because many of my clients cancelled our cleaning service. The business struggled, and I worried it would collapse, leaving us broke.

One way Tom coped with the tension was by listening to audiobooks on his iPhone. Most of the time he walked around the house wearing headphones and he kept them on when we cleaned properties together. There was very little time when Tom and his headphones were apart. I didn't know what he was listening to, but it was his escape and he seemed happy and relaxed, so I said nothing about it.

That's until one morning during winter when I started

the car to warm it up for the kids before I drove them to school. A couple of my staff were in the car with me. Suddenly, explicit sexual content blasted from the car's loudspeakers. Deeply embarrassed, I turned off the sound.

When I was alone with Tom later that morning, I asked him whether he listened to pornography.

'No, no, it must be one of the staff,' he said.

'Are you sure? I don't think anyone was listening to anything when I turned the car ignition on.'

Two days later, Tom admitted the sexual content came from his audiobook. 'The Bluetooth must have kicked in from my iPhone,' he smirked.

Tom's sexual fantasies soared after listening to the audiobooks. His libido intensified so much that I just felt like a prop for his obscene fantasies. To keep the peace and have a happy life I said, 'Okay, let's just do it.' It wasn't me he was doing it to, it was a fantasy based on the lurid stories he listened to. It got so bad that he started counting how often we had sex. Often, he would grab my vagina in front of the kids. When I told him to stop doing it, his response floored me: 'Why? I'm allowed to.'

Tom said if I didn't give him control of our sex life, our relationship was over. I stupidly went along with it. I felt sick to the stomach with what he wanted to do in bed. It wasn't me he wanted; he used me to carry out his fantasies. I felt disgusting, but I thought if it kept the peace for a week, I had to do it.

Tom no longer seemed able to separate reality and fantasy. The line was becoming blurred, and he was finding it difficult to switch from one state to the other. When I asked him to take off his headphones at the dinner table, it was like he was losing something. He was losing himself in the real world and his fantasy world was taking over.

Around this time, I noticed that Tom's lies were becoming more grandiose, especially the stories he told our family and friends about our wealth. Through my behaviour I tried to show him what genuine love was, and that he didn't need to buy love by fabricating stories about our possessions. I wanted to show him that love is acceptance and forgiveness and not about how much money you've got in the bank or what model of car you drive.

Tom truly believed his fantasies, particularly that he'd lost $15 million. Also, that he owned a house in Adelaide next-door to Lleyton Hewitt. That's where I didn't fit in with him. I maybe ticked a couple of boxes, but I wasn't part of his fantasy. I believe that's one reason for the arguments and constant belittling. In Tom's mind, I was wrong for him. I was a bad person. The confusing thing was that having said that, he could be loving, kind, generous, patient and funny. That's what I loved about him.

I think Tom was a bit like me, in that we pretend that we are positive. We both act as if nothing bothers us and everything in life is fine. But like an iceberg, beneath the surface, there is a tremendous amount going on. Tom and I both have our fair share of demons, and maybe we clashed because of our difficult childhoods.

From about mid-2020, Tom's controlling behaviour and violence towards me escalated. I called the police in September 2020, and they removed him from the property. As the police guided Tom into their car, he turned around and glared at me.

'You need to go to counselling,' he shouted. 'You're ruining this relationship.'

Shortly afterwards, I decided to see a counsellor because I kept having panic attacks and felt constantly on edge. The counsellor said one reason for my anxiety was the way Tom treated me. Deep down, I knew she was right, but I didn't want to accept her explanation because I was in love with Tom. Yes, there were bad times and plenty of red flags, but I brushed them aside. I kept hoping I could save Tom from his demons. My philosophy is that everything can be fixed, including people. I kept encouraging Tom to see a counsellor but each time I mentioned it he would fob me off, claiming he was okay and that I was the problem. Whenever this happened, I tried to convince myself that I should accept Tom the way he was.

I have never been one to give up when the going gets tough, yet I feel that approach has not served me well. Years ago, I was chatting with my stepfather.

'Why do you always seem to make the right decision?' I asked.

'I don't always make the right decision,' he said, 'but when I make a decision, good or bad, I stick to it.'

I have questioned many of my decisions and yes, there have been some pretty stupid and regretful ones, but, like Dad and unknowingly, I stuck to them, the good and the bad. I feel like all I've done is go through life thinking that I am lower than anyone. That everybody knows better than me.

In mid-October 2020 my biological father took his own life. I had spent several months prior liaising with his doctors and mental health team in the UK and thought he was improving, but in the end, he hanged himself. I was devastated and wished I had been in England because that might have stopped my father from taking his life. Although my stepfather had been my de facto father since I was six months old, I still loved my biological father and wished I had been able to help him.

At the end of 2020, Tom and I went away for the weekend with our staff for our annual Christmas party. We arranged for a friend to look after the kids and our pets. We'd booked a three-bedroom apartment, and Tom and I stayed there on the Friday night before our staff arrived the next day. It was a terrific weekend and Tom and I got along well. Our landlord had organised for some trees to be delivered to our place on the Friday morning and he asked Tom to water them. When we arrived home on Sunday morning, our landlord was waiting for us at home.

I ran inside to see Daniel and Sophie, but I heard our landlord say: 'Tom, what's happened to my trees. They're all dry.'

While upstairs I heard Tom yelling 'fuck off'. I ran outside to see what was happening. Tom had pushed our landlord to the ground, and they were wrestling. Tom told me his version of the story.

'No, Tom, that's not what happened,' our landlord insisted.

The landlord called the police and made a statement. For once someone else was the target of Tom's violence and it wasn't me imagining it.

Doing the unthinkable

On Friday 15 January 2021, I woke up at four o'clock in the morning. I loved it when the house was quiet, so I sat on the back deck enjoying an espresso and a cigarette, before getting on with some work.

All too soon, the early morning serenity ended when Tom stormed onto the deck in a fury.

I looked up from my work while stubbing out the cigarette. 'What's the matter?'

'You and Joanne were taking the piss out of me yesterday at work,' Tom whined. 'I want to get rid of Joanne.'

'Look, Tom, she was only joking with you, like she always does.'

'No, I don't think it's joking. You were both paying me out.'

'Okay, look, I'll sort it out. I'll tell Joanne to stop teasing you.'

Tom was in an ugly mood for the rest of the day. He was saying some irrational things.

'What are you on about?' I asked. 'Calm down, Tom.'

'I want to get rid of her,' he roared, before swearing at

me and calling me disgusting names that I won't repeat here.

Crashing down, down, down, I felt something inside me slam shut. I switched off, unable to take anymore abuse.

The next morning, Tom smiled his sweetest smile and reached out to me. 'Hey, come here, give us a hug.'

I felt my insides curdle. 'I don't want to.'

'Oh, so you're going to carry this on, are you?' he sneered.

'You called me an effing C**T, you know I hate that. Why did you do that?'

'Oh God, if you're going to keep it going, I'll go downstairs.' He turned away from me and adjusted his headphones.

I followed him. 'Do you want any help?'

'No!'

Usually on a Saturday night we were intimate, but that night I didn't want to do anything.

'Do you mind if we're not intimate tonight?' I asked.

'Oh, so you don't want to do anything?'

'No, I'm not feeling like it. I just want to chill out and watch a bit of TV. Is that all right?'

'All right then,' he sighed. 'I'll do something myself.'

I cooked dinner, and we sat at the dining table with the kids. But Tom didn't touch his food. Instead, he glanced at his dinner, stared at the television for long periods without speaking, then looked down at his plate again. He had a scary vacant look in his eyes.

'Are you all right?' I asked, worried that something was seriously wrong with Tom.

'Yep, I'm fine.'

After dinner, I got the kids ready for bed.

'Sophie can sleep with you,' Tom said. 'I'll sleep in her room because I want to do something tonight.'

I put Sophie in my bed, then returned to the lounge room to watch television. About 8.30 pm, Tom announced he was going to bed. Shortly after 10 o'clock, while I watched the end of a TV program, Tom stormed into the lounge room. He stood between me and the television.

'The reason you're so tired and neglect me is you stay up all night watching TV,' he growled.

I felt the blood drain from me. Tom walked outside for a cigarette, and I turned off the TV. I realised I couldn't do it anymore. I couldn't live with this man who treated me like shit.

The next day when I got up, I told Tom I was going for a walk. While wandering down our street and onto the main road, I thought, I'm done. I'm done.

When I returned, Tom acted as though there was no problem. 'Are we going to talk or what?' he asked.

'When you say you want to talk, it means I've got to listen to you,' I said. 'There's no point in talking.'

He lost his temper.

To avoid a fight, I started cleaning our en-suite bathroom. Tom followed me. While I was cleaning the toilet, he lurched towards me.

'Fuck off!' I shrieked.

Tom pushed me against the bathroom wall then grabbed my head and pushed it deep into the bowl of the toilet.

'Piss off,' I screamed.

He left the bathroom, and I escaped to our bedroom. I sat on the bed panicking and wondering what to do. Tom returned.

'Get the fuck away from me,' I gasped.

He pushed me onto the bed and raised his fist to hit me. Sophie and Daniel were in the kitchen, and I called out to them: 'Kids, please phone the police.'

Tom left the bedroom. I heard him say: 'Mummy's gone crazy. Mummy's not well. She thinks I've hurt her. I haven't touched her.'

When I left the bedroom, Daniel and Sophie ran up to me. 'Why are you asking us to phone the police? Daddy didn't do anything to you.'

'Get out of the house,' Tom raged.

I knew I had to telephone the police, but I knew there

was something inside me that was saying, if I phone the police, there's no turning back. This is it. I've had enough. I was empty, I had nothing left to give.

I went to my office and looked up an Airbnb for me and the kids to go to. Almost immediately, Tom strolled into the room.

'If you take the kids, I'll report you for kidnapping,' he threatened. 'I want you to get out of here and take a breather for a few hours. But while you've gone, I'm going to report you as an unfit mother with mental health issues.'

In that moment something in me snapped. I was done. I knew Tom was my partner and the father of my children, but nothing else. I don't know what it is in me that I find it hard to walk away from people who hurt me. My mum left me all the time, but I had promised myself that I would never be the one to leave. People leave me, but I don't leave them. Still, I knew that was my only remaining option. I knew I was finished with Tom and his abuse.

I had reached the point where I felt the only solution was to separate and to only allow contact with Tom via a mediator. I had been mulling over this idea for a long time but hesitated to put it into action because I knew Tom adored Sophie and Daniel and they loved him. I didn't want to hurt Tom or the kids.

I felt bad about what I was about to do, but I could no longer trust Tom. I never wanted to talk to him without a mediator being present because I knew from his usual behaviour that he would try to control me, manipulate me, lie to me and threaten me. He would never leave me in peace.

'I'll never trust you ever again,' I cried, before phoning the police. The police officer asked me whether Tom had assaulted me. I had an out-of-body experience and thought I would say 'no', but I couldn't stop myself from saying 'yes'. At last, I had done it! When the police arrived, I told them Tom needed psych help urgently.

'I don't want him to get into trouble,' I pleaded. 'He's not well and needs to see a mental health team.'

'We have to charge him because he assaulted you,' the police officer said. They took him away.

When Tom returned from the police station on the Sunday afternoon, I packed some clothes for him, and he left the house to stay with a friend. On the Wednesday he posted a YouTube video declaring his intention to end his life. He repeated the comment five times. In his statement to the police, Tom had admitted he assaulted me on the Sunday, but he denied it in the YouTube video.

On Thursday morning Tom and I were due in court, but he turned up at home, breaching the intervention order. I was terrified. In front of our children, he announced he was planning to go off and enjoy himself for a few days. 'I'm going to have all the sex I want, then end my life,' he snarled.

I was aghast and didn't know where to turn or what to do.

The following Sunday night, Tom posted another video on YouTube. I didn't watch it, but hundreds of people did and so did the police. In that second video Tom described in graphic detail how he planned to end his life.

After posting the second video to YouTube, Tom telephoned one of my staff members. As soon as Tom ended the call, she phoned. She was sobbing, so much so that I found it difficult to understand her.

'Tom needs you to find him because he's going to hang himself in 20 minutes if you don't,' she screamed, her usual calm demeanour replaced by panic.

In my own wave of panic, I put the children to bed. Then the police phoned me, saying they were on their way. I was terrified, I did not know what was happening. A few minutes later, three squad cars showed up, and the police searched for Tom. When they found him, they took him to hospital. That night I spoke with the mental health team, and they assured me they would look after Tom. They too had seen both his YouTube videos.

At 10 o'clock a police officer called me. 'Don't worry, Leena,' he said reassuringly. 'We're not charging him with anything. This is all about mental health right now.'

The following morning at six o'clock, the police phoned. 'Last night the mental health team discharged Tom from hospital, and he spent the night with us at the police station. We've charged him with breaching the IVO and bailed him to Canberra.'

I was horrified. The mental health team should never have let him go. There must be a massive change to the way we assess people's mental health. A questionnaire with responses ranging from one to 10 asking how someone feels isn't enough. If someone doesn't think there's anything wrong with them, they won't say, 'I'm feeling a one or a two on the scale.' They're going to say, '10, 10, 10, 10, 10.' And that should raise red flags. If someone says that to the mental health team their alarm bells should ring. Because it's not real.

The police should never have bailed Tom to drive all the way to Canberra because he hadn't slept for several days. In his sleep-deprived state he drove to Canberra and stayed with an old school friend.

The next day I noticed a $70 payment from a boat, camping and fishing shop in Canberra appear on our credit card statement. I wondered what Tom had bought. Little did I know the devastating impact that $70 would have on so many of our lives.

A few days later, Tom publicly announced on Facebook that he was planning to end his life. As he did in his YouTube video, he described how he would do it. The worst part is he claimed he was going to do it on Daniel's tenth birthday. I couldn't believe he could be so cruel to our son. They adored each other. To threaten to kill himself was unthinkable, but to do it on Daniel's birthday was too horrific to comprehend.

On Friday afternoon, Tom sent me an explicit email. In it he described in precise detail how he would end his life. I screamed and started shaking, then phoned the police. The duty officer told me someone would call me. I waited and waited.

Suddenly, the phone rang, but to my dismay it was Tom. I was too frightened to answer his call and let it ring out because I was still waiting for the police to phone me. I didn't know what to do and telephoned a friend.

'I need you,' I whimpered, collapsing into a heap on the floor.

My friend came over, and she arranged for someone to pick up Daniel and Sophie from school.

My friends were comforting me when two police officers arrived. They introduced themselves politely. I thought they would update me on where Matt was and the police's plan.

I have never been so wrong.

The next words I heard were going to change my children's and my life forever.

'I'm sorry, Leena, but Tom has passed away,' one police officer said.

The second officer nodded, adding: 'This was a final 'Fuck You' from him to you.'

A final thought...

Telling my kids their dad had gone to the stars was truly the most traumatic thing I have ever done. To see their trusting faces looking at me, not knowing what I was about to say, and me knowing that what I was about to say was going to break their little hearts and change their lives forever. Daniel and Sophie are my world and I do everything I can to protect them from pain. But I feel like all I've done is give them pain, pain that will mark their future.

Maybe if I had left Tom when the red flags first appeared I could have prevented his children from losing their father? Or if I had left him that last time he gave me a black eye? Or the time before? I feel so much guilt that staying in the relationship might have contributed to Tom's passing. I can't stop thinking of all the things I could have done to prevent a fatherless future for my precious children.

Why didn't I leave? That question swirls around my head and torments me at all hours of the day and night. The physical abuse was difficult to bear, but once the black eyes and bruises disappeared, the pain passed. But the psychological abuse, which was subtle and highly manipulative, strips you of your self-esteem, your confidence, and your ability to trust your instinct and to act on it. The trauma of it all will continue for many years to come. In many respects Tom's premeditated suicide is a form of domestic violence because it is keeping me and my kids in a deep dark place. I don't want that for any of us. I don't want it for you and urge you to take action.

I suppose you'll say you can't leave because your situation is complex, and the good days make up for the bad ones. From my own experience I know that some days are calm, and your relationship feel as if it is on an even keel. You guiltily push away thoughts of leaving, hoping the good days will last. But they don't. We all know that. Please don't be like me and leave it until it is too late.

I long for more people to leave at the red flag stage before the bad days start. I don't want what happened to me and my children to occur to anyone else. It's vital to seek help if you have a partner who abuss you. There are a raft of organisations providing support for victims of physical and psychological abuse and I've included contact details at the end of this book.

Please act on the red flags as soon as you notice them rather than being like me and making excuses or brushing them aside. Please don't think, like I did, that you can 'fix' your abusive partner or save them from their demons.

I'm still trying to come to terms with why I stayed with Tom when there were so many red flags. I don't want to tell you what to do because my father, ex-husband and Tom all controlled my life, and I don't want to do that to you. But leaving is your choice, a choice I urge you to make if your partner abuses you physically or psychologically.

Please don't be afraid to tell someone you are not okay. You have a strong voice and I urge you to speak up about what's going on in your life. But be selective about who you tell, limiting it to trusted confidantes who won't judge you.

I hope your decision to leave has been brought forward by reading my story of love and loss. Please listen to your instincts, trust your judgement and have the strength to stand up and say, 'No, I will not put up with this.'

Sharing my learnings
with you

Thank you for reading my story. I hope it helps you to make the decisions I didn't make in time. Since Tom's death I've been having regular counselling and it is helping me to better understand myself, my relationship and why I didn't leave before it was too late.

Through counselling and reading everything I can get my hands on, I now have a name for what I experienced— gaslighting, coercion, controlling, manipulation and domestic abuse. I wish someone had told me about these forms of abuse years ago—I wrongly thought I was imagining them and it was all in my head. Now I feel compelled to share my learnings with you to help you understand what might be happening in your relationship.

In the following pages I describe several types of domestic abuse and ways of responding to it. I'm on a steep learning curve and am not an expert, so in places I've summarised articles from the experts. I've provided the original source of the articles so you can easily find them on the internet and begin your own journey of discovery. When I first read these articles, it was like a light bulb exploded in my head because they precisely described my situation and experiences. I could see myself in them and shuddered with the feeling of recognition.

In other places I describe the insights I've gained through counselling and I track my journey of healing. It is a bumpy ride but I hope that by sharing my innermost thoughts and feelings it will help you to learn about domestic abuse, how to escape from it and the roller coaster of emotions you might go through on the pathway out of an abusive relationship.

My goal now is to share these learnings with you, hoping it will help you to make the decisions I wasn't confident enough to take.

What does domestic abuse look like?

DOMESTIC VIOLENCE GROOMING

KNOW THE SIGNS!

When I read an article in MINDJournal about grooming as a prelude to domestic abuse my heart skipped a beat. *How domestic abusers groom and isolate their victims* describes exactly what happened in my relationship[1].

The article said abusers often come on strong with intense romance.

That's what happened for me.

He came on too strong, too quickly.

But I ignored the red flags.

Then the intimidation starts

Romantic gestures can soon become intimidation.

Abusers blame their partners for growing tensions.

Victims try to appease their abuser and return to the romantic phase.

Grooming family and friends

Abusers often groom friends, family and others to overlook the signs of abuse and cut ties with the victim.

Abusers are charming and helpful to family and friends to disarm them, who have a very different experience of the abuser to that of the victim.

Be on the alert for signs of grooming

If you suspect that someone is grooming you or another person, please contact a domestic violence hotline for advice on how to respond to it.

---

[1] https://themindsjournal.com/domestic-abusers-groom-isolate-victims/

**THERE ARE FOUR STAGES
IN THE CYCLE OF ABUSE**

**TENSION BUILDING, INCIDENT,
RECONCILIATION, CALM**

Understanding the cycle of abuse

Crystal Raypole wrote about the cycle of abuse in a Healthline article on the internet.[2] Reading this article helped me to understand why I didn't leave. Raypole said one of the reasons many victims choose to stay with their abusers is the cycle of abuse, which has four stages: building of tension, the abuse incident, reconciliation and a period of calm.

The Building of Tension

I was interested to learn from Raypole that abusers harm their victims because they are in a stressful situation and that potential stressors include fatigue, physical illness, work problems and family issues. I was stopped in my tracks when I read that when stressed, the abuser will start exhibiting signs of paranoia, anger, injustice and powerlessness. That's exactly what happened in my relationship.

The Abusive Incident

After the build-up of tension, the next step of the cycle is the abusive incident, which can take the form of emotional manipulation, sexual or physical violence, attempts to control the behaviour of the victim, threats of property destruction or harm, or name-calling or insults. I was horrified to read this list because every item was ever-present in my relationship.

Reconciliation

After the abusive incident, many couples experience a period of reconciliation. An abuser might be loving and kind or give the victim a gift to make up for the abuse. This didn't happen in my relationship. Instead, my partner blamed me for triggering his abuse. Still, I know it does occur in many relationships and according to Raypole it is because our brains release oxytocin and dopamine. When this happens, it gives the victim hope that the relationship will survive and they are more likely to want to stay.

---

[2] https://www.healthline.com/health/relationships/cycle-of-abuse

Calm

The abusive partner is likely to try to justify why the abuse happened by apologising in such a way that it minimises the victim's perception of their responsibility for what occurred. Raypole said some of the ways an abuser might establish a period of calm are by:

- Using outside factors as a reason for their behaviour

- Apologising but blaming others at the same time

- Denying or minimising the abuse itself

- Saying it's your fault because you provoked them.

Sadly, the calm period is usually short-lived and once external stressors come in, they can set off the abuser again.

Domestic Abuse Is Not Just Physical.

Domestic Abuse Is Not Just Leaving Physical Scars.

Domestic Abuse Is Isolating.

Domestic Abuse Is Debilitating.

Domestic Abuse Can Leave Deep Emotional Scars.

Types of domestic abuse

GASLIGHTING

TO MANIPULATE (SOMEONE) BY PSYCHOLOGICAL MEANS INTO DOUBTING THEIR OWN SANITY

My counsellor taught me about gaslighting. I had never heard about it before and wish I had known about this practice years ago because it would have saved me a lot of grief. I am not an expert on gaslighting, so here I am presenting details of the tactic from an article I read by Jennifer Huizen in *Medical News Today*.[3]

Gaslighting is a form of abuse where the victim is manipulated into doubting their own sanity. In her article, Jennifer Huizen said that according to the National Domestic Violence Hotline in America, techniques an abuser might use to gaslight include the following:[4]

Countering
Countering describes an abuser questioning the victim's memories.

Withholding
Jennifer Huizen said withholding involves refusing to engage in a conversation. An abuser using this technique might pretend not to understand the victim so they don't have to respond to them.

Trivialising
According to Jennifer Huizen, trivialising occurs when an abuser belittles or disregards the victim's feelings. They might accuse them of being too sensitive or of overreacting when they have valid concerns and feelings.

Denial
Denial involves an abuser pretending to forget events or how they occurred. They might deny having said or done something or accuse the victim of making things up.

Diverting
When a gaslighter employs diverting techniques, they change the focus of a discussion and question the victim's credibility.

---

[3] https://www.medicalnewstoday.com/articles/gaslighting
[4] https://www.thehotline.org/resources/what-is-gaslighting

CONTROLLING AND COERCIVE BEHAVIOUR

THE 12 SIGNS

One of the tactics abusers often use is control and coercion of the victim. Abusers might control a victim by limiting access to money or monitoring all communication. In a 2019 Healthline article, 'How to identify coercive control', Cindy Lamothe outlined 12 major signs of coercive control, along with some resources to help victims of coercion.[5]

Isolating you from your support system

In her article, Lamothe included comments about coercive control by the clinical psychologist Dr Cali Estes. Dr Este said a controlling partner will try to cut you off from friends and family or limit contact with them so you don't receive the support you need. That's what my partner did to me. Dr Estes outlined a few ways abusers do this:

- Suggesting shared phone and social media accounts for convenience

- Moving you far away from your family so that it's hard to visit them

- Fabricating lies about you to others

- Monitoring all your phone calls with your family and cutting the line off if anyone tries to intervene

- Convincing you that your family hates you and doesn't want to talk to you.

Monitoring your activity throughout the day

Lamothe quoted Dr Wendy L. Patrick, an expert in criminal law, who maintains that abusers pursue coercive control through attempts to make themselves omnipresent. They do this by wiring the house with cameras or recording devices.

'This invasive surveillance often extends to private areas, such as the bedroom and even the bathroom,'

---

[5] https://www.healthline.com/health/coercive-control

Patrick notes, 'adding an element of humiliation to what is already a clear boundary violation.'

Cindy Lamothe said these techniques give the abuser an added element of control and also serves as a reminder to the victim that they're watching.

Denying you freedom and autonomy
Someone exerting coercive control might try to control your freedom of movement and independence by:

- Not allowing you to go to work or school

- Restricting your access to transport

- Stalking you when you're out

- Taking your phone and changing all your passwords.

Gaslighting
Dr Cali Estes notes that the abuser must always be right, and they will force the victim to acknowledge this. They will manipulate, lie and gaslight to get their way and convince the victim that they are wrong.

Name-calling and putting you down
Dr Melissa Hamilton, a criminologist and expert in domestic abuse, said malicious put-downs, name-calling and frequent criticisms are all forms of bullying behaviour designed to make you feel unimportant and deficient. As you read in my story, this daily abuse by my former partner destroyed my confidence and sense of self-worth.

Limiting your access to money
According to Lamothe, controlling finances is a way an abuser restricts a victim's freedom and ability to leave the relationship. Some examples of how an abuser tries to exert financial control include:

- Placing you on a strict budget that barely covers the basics

- Limiting your access to bank accounts

- Hiding financial resources

- Preventing you from having a credit card

- Rigorously monitoring what you spend.

Reinforcing traditional gender roles

Many abusers try to make a distinction between who functions as the man and the woman in the relationship. They'll attempt to justify that women are homemakers and mothers, while men are the breadwinners. Using this argument, they may coerce a female victim into doing all the cleaning, cooking and childcare.

Turning your kids against you

Abusers often try to weaponise the victim's children against them by telling the children the victim is a bad parent or belittling them in front of the children.

Controlling aspects of your health and body

Abusers often monitor and control how much the victim eats or sleeps. They might even force the victim to count calories after every meal or adhere to a strict exercise regimen.

Making accusations

Many abusers try to limit the victim's contact with family and friends by complaining about the amount of time the victim spends with those close to them.

Regulating your sexual relationship

Abusers might make demands about the amount of times they have sex with the victim each week and the kinds of activities they perform. They may also demand to take sexual pictures or videos of the victim or refuse to wear a condom.

Dr Melissa Hamilton says: 'The victims may come to an "understanding" that if they do not comply with their perpetrators' demands or desires, they may face significant consequences.'

Threatening your children or pets

According to Dr Hamilton, if physical, emotional, or financial threats don't work as desired, an abuser may try to use threats against others in an attempt to control the victim. Examples include:

- Making violent threats against them

- Threatening to call social services and say you're neglecting or abusing your children when you aren't

- Intimidating you by threatening to make important decisions about your kids without your consent

- Threatening to kidnap your children or get rid of your pet.

An abuser will always blame you for their abusive actions.

I have been blamed for every abusive word and action, and I would try and defend myself because deep down, I knew I didn't do anything to deserve the abuse.

In the end, I would give in and be so careful as to what I said, what I did, basically walking on egg shells and giving in to his demands.

However, he would move the goal posts all the time, twist the details of his demands to the point where they were unachievable.

This then gave him reason to lash out and berate me.

There is no compromising with an abuser.

Peace within an abusive relationship is very short-lived.

The abuser gets a sick pleasure in seeing you distressed, racked with anxiety and confusion.

The abuser does not want a resolution.

They want to torment you and will never stop.

**BULLYING OF ANY KIND
IN A RELATIONSHIP**

IS ABUSE

Abuse is not limited to intimate or personal relationships.

Bullying is rife in so many other forms.

The workplace: Gossiping, undermining, name calling, intimidating, ridiculing and mocking.

Social Media: Negatively commenting, stalking, threatening, demeaning and name calling.

Friendships: Back stabbing, gossiping, name calling and hurtful teasing.

Gossip can be damaging.

Name calling can be hurtful and demeaning.

Intimidation can cause anxiety.

To put a stop to this and break the cycle, change starts with YOU.

Don't engage in negative gossip.

Turn negative remarks into positive conversation.

Set an example and be the better person.

Tell your boss/supervisor/administrator.

Keep your private life private.

Don't trust easily.

Stand up for yourself.

Enough is enough!

MICROMANAGING

TO MANAGE WITH EXCESSIVE CONTROL

Signs of micromanaging

- Blame for errors.

- Criticism of ability.

- Insults and put-downs.

- Discounting or denial of accomplishments.

- Exclusion, icing-out.

- Yelling, screaming.

- Stealing credit.

WHEN YOUR GOOD ENOUGH

WILL NEVER BE ENOUGH

'What could I do to make you stop the name-calling?'

Nothing.

'Will you ever care enough about me to stop hurting me?'

No.

'Will changing make you love me?'

No.

'Would loving you harder make you love me more?'

No.

'When will my good enough will be enough?'

Never.

When should I walk away from you?

Now.

IT HURTS TO FEEL UNLOVED

EXCRUCIATING TO BE TOLD
YOU'RE UNLOVEABLE

There are no limits to the levels of hurt an abuser will go to.

Every word is meant to emotionally and mentally destroy you.

ABUSERS ARE MASTERS OF DISGUISE

NOT ALL IS AS IT SEEMS...

Abusers are serial manipulators and masters of disguise.

This is how they are able to segregate you from family and friends.

They act in one way with family and friends and in the community but behave very differently behind closed doors.

Those on the outside see a very different person to the one you claim abuses you.

Even when the relationship has ended in any way, the manipulation continues, either within the community, social media or by friends/family of the abuser.

How wrong is the childhood chant 'Sticks and stones may beak my bones but words will never hurt me'?

Sticks and stones may leave visible scars but you don't see the scars that have been caused by the name calling, the threats, the gaslighting, the criticism and belittling.

It all hurts!

It all leaves scars!

It all has to stop!

TOO EMOTIONALLY PARALYSED

TO LEAVE AN ABUSIVE RELATIONSHIP

During my 13-year relationship I felt too emotionally paralysed to leave.

Over the years there were moments when I should have left.

It's such a surreal feeling.

You know leaving is the right thing to do.

But you stay.

You know things will never change.

But you stay.

You know it takes that one brave step to break free.

But you can't.

You've been prevented from expressing your feelings so often you just don't feel or think like you used to.

I remember a numbing feeling on my forehead as I tried to resolve each argument.

At the same time, I tried to sift through the irrational vitriol coming out of his mouth.

Everything shut down.

I would walk away from him.

He would follow me, screaming and yelling.

Despite my pleas to leave me alone, he never did.

I was backed into a corner every single time.

In response, I would shut down.

It was too hard to try to compromise because he refused to listen.

I would sit there and hear him but not listen because every part of me was emotionally paralysed.

I don't know if I will ever regain full feelings again.

SEE BELOW FOR THE TOP EXCUSE FOR DOMESTIC VIOLENCE

Still looking for the top excuse for domestic violence? You can stop now.

There isn't a top excuse.

There is NO excuse.

SOMETIMES YOU GET TO A PLACE WHERE YOU ARE JUST SO BROKEN

THAT CHANGE IS THE ONLY OPTION

Escaping an abusive relationship

I wish I had read Cindy Lamothe's Healthline article about abusive relationships years ago. Cindy interviewed several domestic abuse experts who suggested ways for victims of coercion to get out of a bad relationship.[6] She notes that safely leaving the relationship can be complex, especially if children are involved, but it is possible to do so with careful planning.

Dr Wendy Patrick recommends that victims maintain close communication with their family, friends and support systems at all times as a safeguard. Other tactics Patrick recommends include:

- Regularly calling a domestic violence hotline

- Practise how to get out safely and teach your kids to identify a safe place, such as a friend's house or the library and how to call the police

- Develop a safety plan that includes where to go and who to stay with.

[6] https://www.healthline.com/health/coercive-control

A JOURNEY STARTS BY PUTTING ONE FOOT IN FRONT OF THE OTHER

BUT SOMETIMES THE FIRST STEP IS ABOUT GETTING ON YOUR FEET

Healing after an abusive relationship

I didn't expect nor want my separated journey to begin this way.

However hard I thought it would be in better circumstances, this was far more traumatic, frightening and upsetting than I ever could have imagined.

I was thrown into the deepest and darkest of waters and while on the surface I seemed to have it together for my children, I was frantically paddling underneath the water to get to shore.

Eventually, my feet reached the sandy shore and I was able to put one foot in front of the other. Some days I take more steps forward than other days, but I force myself to keep walking, one step at a time.

TRAUMA TRIGGERS

A STIMULUS THAT SETS OFF
A MEMORY OF TRAUMA

Trauma triggers have become daily life for me.

The triggers can be so small, but the effect is the same as the day of the original trauma.

The initial trigger sometimes leads me on to additional triggers because there were so many traumatic and abusive events.

I work very hard to not let myself be triggered because it's like reliving it all over again and I never want to be in that place again.

This is supposed to be the time where I rebuild myself and get back to some normality, but I fear it's going to take a very long time to get there.

Flashbacks are relentless. I am beginning to wonder if they will ever stop.

Too many reminders of what was and the final chapter that saw an end to 13 years of turmoil.

There are moments where I miss him and then I remind myself that although time is easing the pain and trauma, it doesn't ease the years of lies, emotional blackmail, physical and mental abuse.

I feel I am still living in the past because for the first time, I have peace.

But it's like coming outside from a loud, thumping nightclub where I can't hear myself speak or thin. The quiet is so extreme I can hear my heartbeat in my ears, feel my body adjusting to the space around me. There's nobody in my face or bumping into me anymore.

Then, along with the quiet, my mind thinks it's playing, rewinding, forwarding pausing a really shitty movie, constantly.

It's exhausting!

HEALING DOESN'T MEAN
THE DAMAGE NEVER EXISTED

IT MEANS THE DAMAGE NO LONGER
CONTROLS YOUR LIFE.

My relationship ended so traumatically, something I did not want.

I somehow found my voice and something inside me took over, and I stood up for myself.

I felt the situation had gone to such a level that I could not sustain it anymore, nor did I want to.

I was scared of the repercussions because he always threatened to burn me or destroy me.

This time, I was more scared to stay.

The damage I sustained over the 13 years—that I allowed to control me—is starting to heal, but I suffer from daily shock waves, panic attacks and anxiety.

However, as you will learn about me soon, I have mastered the ability to deflect with humour and put my brave face on over the years, hiding the raging pain and despair inside me.

I am trying to gain control over my life, for my children's lives, in the hope for a brighter, calmer future.

It's bloody hard, but thanks to my small circle of friends and family, my *Tears of a Clown* Facebook page and regular counselling, I am heading in the right direction.

Why do we grieve the loss of an abusive relationship?

Vision Psychology in Brisbane published an article on the internet that helped me to understand why I'm grieving the end of such a toxic and abusive relationship.[7] Reading the article was a lightbulb moment for me. It states that when an abusive relationship comes to an end, the grief can be intense and all-consuming.

This article resonated with me because I still struggle with the conflicting parts of my former partner's behaviour. On the one hand, he could be loving and caring, but more often than not he was mean and abusive.

Vision Psychology said the intense grief and emotional roller coaster results from the co-existence of fear, pain and disappointment as well as love, kindness and hope in the same relationship.

'Abusive relationships are often not bad all the time,' the article stated. 'There are often good moments. These moments are real, and it's very normal to have positive and loving feelings for someone in these moments. When the abusive relationship comes to an end, it is not just the abusive, painful moments that come to an end, it is also the loss of the loving, caring and romantic moments. It is very normal to feel loss and sadness when we lose someone that we love—even if there are bits of them that we hate or fear, or that may actually even be dangerous.'

Vision Psychology said that to move on, you will need to gain insight into the dynamics and the cycle of abuse, your own internal thought processes and feelings, and the fears and the vulnerabilities that allowed you to become entangled in an abusive relationship. Importantly, it stated that it is important to validate your feelings of loss, fear and uncertainty, and to have self-compassion for the losses you have suffered; to find empathy and support from

---

[7] https://www.visionpsychology.com/grief-after-an-abusive-relationship

loved ones or a professional person who can guide you through the process of grief and dealing with the trauma.

What stands out to me the most from the Vision Psychology article is the following statement: 'As you grieve the loss of an abusive relationship, you are grieving the loss of a romantic dream/vision—but you can find hope of a new dream/vision.'

This gives me hope.

GRIEF DOES NOT COMMAND PITY

IT REQUESTS ACKNOWLEDGMENT

Grief can be very confusing, especially when we find ourselves grieving for the end of a toxic relationship.

Each memory that pops up, whether painful or joyful, is an opportunity to either push it away or acknowledge it.

In order to heal, we need to face our demons and grief takes us down that path whether we like it or not.

I have fought my grief because I didn't understand why I was grieving for someone who was so nasty, manipulative and abusive to me.

I am now accepting the memories and the grief more, but it is still extremely difficult.

EMOTIONAL AND PSYCHOLOGICAL TRAUMA

CAN CAUSE PHYSICAL SYMPTOMS

Emotional, mental and psychological abuse affects our physical body.

I was always in pain.

I didn't realise it at the time, but every muscle and nerve hurt because I was always tense.

Being tense all the time is exhausting and therefore I was always tired.

I had countless visits to doctors and blood test after blood test to figure out what was wrong with me.

Now, my physical ailments are decreasing.

My energy has increased.

I feel lighter.

Still so far to go, but questions are being answered.

I AM TIRED OF FIGHTING

I JUST WANT TO BE FOUGHT FOR...

REOCCURRING NIGHTMARES

SO REAL ARE HIS ACTIONS AND ANGER... AND MY FEAR...

Last night's nightmare was up there for being the worst I've ever experienced.

He was in my house, chasing after me and destroying everything in his path.

Nothing could stop him from trying to get to me and hurt me.

He kicked and bashed down walls and doors.

He picked up and broke my most treasured possessions, knowing what they meant to me.

He was raging like a wild angry bull.

He was verbally threatening, saying he would destroy me.

He was screaming at me with intense hatred.

Then the police arrived.

One officer came up to me and said: 'You're safe now.'
The policeman asked me if I was okay.
I looked up and asked him to hold and protect me.
He did.
I physically felt the officer's arms around me and I truly felt safe.
No longer alone to fight the abuse, anger and vitriol.
This was only a dream but it was my reality for 13 years.
The only thing that is not real is my feeling of being safe and protected.

I THINK I'M AN INTELLIGENT PERSON

SO... HOW COULD I BE SO STUPID?

I always thought I could stand up for myself.

I always thought I knew when someone was lying to me.

I always thought I was stubborn enough to stick to my guns.

If I was a good friend to myself, I would have taken myself aside and not left until I saw sense!

Respect for someone is based on:
Morals.
Values.
Communication.
Trust.
Accountability.
Boundaries.

Respect has to work both ways because if it isn't, then that's when you start to compromise and the downward spiral begins.

LEARNING HOW TO RESPECT YOURSELF AGAIN

IT'S HARD AND TAKES SO MUCH TIME

Self-respect is holding yourself in esteem and believing you are good and worthy of being treated well.[8]

An example of self-respect is when you know you deserve to be treated right and, as a result, you do not tolerate others lying to you or treating you unfairly.

I have started to learn how to respect myself again—it's four steps forward and two steps back.

For so long, I have believed that I am worthless, useless and doubted myself in everything.

It's going to take a lot of time, but I've taken the first steps.

---

[8] https://www.yourdictionary.com/self-respect

I WISH I COULD BELIEVE IN LOVE

SO I AM TRYING TO LOVE MYSELF AGAIN...

I used to love the idea of meeting someone and falling in love.

Now my trust and faith in finding love is near on non-existent.

I have accepted that I will never be able to trust another man ever again... no matter what they say or do.

So, I now know that I am destined to live my life solo and that's okay.

I am so lucky to not only have one true love but two—my children.

After reading my story, I think you will agree with me that my sole purpose in life is to be a good mother and to love, nurture and protect my children with everything I have.

COUNSELLING YOUR KID(S) THROUGH TRAUMA

WHEN YOU'RE NOT A COUNSELLOR = WINGING IT!

Parenting during normal day to day life is not easy but trying to support, comfort and repair your kid(s) from trauma is unbelievably difficult.

As much as some of us parents aren't doctors, nurses, chefs or teachers, some of us aren't counsellors or psychologists.

But, like most parents, we know our kids, we love our kids and ultimately, we do the best for our kids.

How do I heal them when I am trying to heal myself?

We heal each other with love, cuddling, laughter and being a family.

How do I wake up every morning, get dressed, put my face on (makeup), make my bed, get breakfast and lunches for the kids and generally go about life as normal?

It's a new normal and while so much has changed, so much hasn't.

Kids need routine and structure because this gives them a feeling of security.

How do I answer their questions about what's happened when I don't have the answers myself?

I tell them that I don't know.

I have to be honest with them.

As a parent, we don't get everything right, but more often than not, we do.

Parenting is winging it every day as life throws us curveballs all the time.

We might look like we have our s**t together but really … we're just winging it!

It's been a challenging week with the three of us struggling with a roller coaster of turbulent emotions.

I regressed with flashbacks.

But I had to put the flashbacks and nightmares aside to help my children deal with their trauma and pain.

I'm spreading myself too thin.

Now it's just me doing everything.

I have no time to catch my breath.

I know I have to take stock.

If I don't look after myself I'll eventually fall apart.

Then I'll be no good for my children.

Easier said than done.

How do I do that?

Becoming a mum, I quickly learned what I want or need comes last to my kids' needs.

Becoming a single parent, I also quickly learned that dealing with my own emotions had to come last.

Everything I do is for my two kids.

My kids are my world.

 And I am their world.

I can't remember the last time I relaxed—I mean totally relaxed.

Years and years of anxiety and trauma have trained my body and mind to never switch off.

I know to be the best parent to my kids I need to work on my mind, body and soul.

KEEP YOUR CIRCLE SMALL

QUALITY OVER QUANTITY

Work out who is loyal to you.
Who can you rely on.
Those who talk about others, will talk about you.
Someone who is supportive and not judgemental.
Someone who makes time for you.
Regain control over your life and who is in it.
Don't feel obligated to anyone outside of your circle.
Keep your circle small.
Confide ONLY in those you trust.
You can't stop gossip BUT you don't have to react to it.
Stay True To Yourself.
Your Personal Life Is Nobody's Business.
Refrain from posting negative comments about your relationship on social media.
Get Professional Support And Counselling.
Focus On You.
Start Healing.

Now I am no longer in a toxic relationship, friends in my small circle are beginning to talk more openly about what they saw and felt was happening in my relationship.

I know I tried to protect my partner and family from onlookers by not telling them what was going on because my partner made me feel I couldn't and wouldn't survive without him.

I believed this.

As the toll on my emotions and mental health grew stronger, I was finding it harder and harder to mask what was going on behind closed doors.

I did not have the energy to pretend we were a happy couple and a solid family unit.

Even on social media, he would sing my praises and declare his love for me when the night before, he hurled abuse at me.

I would be invited to functions, parties and dinners and I would accept, but then cancel at the last minute because something had happened or I just couldn't face anyone.

If you have a gut feeling your friend or someone you know is potentially in a toxic relationship, please keep track of the excuses and reasons for cancelling.

There could be a lot more going on than meets the eye.

BROKEN PEOPLE

SAVE BROKEN PEOPLE

It is bittersweet to share your story with someone who has walked a similar path or is as broken as you.

There's nothing quite like 'I get you,' or 'I understand, I've been there.'

No-one's life story or experiences are the same as anyone else's.

A bit like a fingerprint, our experiences are unique to us.

Talking is as important as listening.

We all want to be heard and listened to but we all must listen to others.

It's a balance: Ying and Yang, checks and balances, give and take.

By talking, you can share the lessons you've learned.

By listening, you can learn about other people's life lessons.

If you have no-one you can turn to—I am here for you.

You are NOT alone!

I will help in any way I can.

I've been there.

It's scary.

It's hard.

But with the right support, this nightmare can end safely and carefully.

Anything you say to me is in complete confidence.

I get it.

I get you.

Please feel welcome to get in touch with me via my *Tears of a Clown* Facebook page:

https://www.facebook.com/TOAC2021

Acknowledgements

I'd like to acknowledge everyone both past and present who has experienced domestic abuse. It's time to speak out and change the future for not only ourselves, but our daughters, sons, and so many others.

For years, my voice was stifled, but some of you knew what was happening without me saying a word. Now, for the first time in my life, I have a voice and I want to be heard. I want others to be heard too.

Although I have much healing to do, part of that healing will be made possible by learning, understanding and sharing information about domestic abuse. My aim is to highlight the red flags and early signs of abuse and encourage you to not discount them the way I did.

To my children, my wish for you is to treat others with kindness and respect. Allow nothing less than kindness and respect for yourselves from others.

Thank you to my small circle of family and friends who have supported me throughout my life. You know who you are, and I will be forever grateful for everything you have done for me, especially for listening to me. You will always be in my heart.

A big thank you to Gabriella who has been so incredible throughout the journey in writing this book. You have been respectful, kind and so supportive. I couldn't have done it without you.

Domestic Violence Hotlines

Australia　　　　Call 1800 737 732

Visit: www.1800respect.org.au

Police: 000 if in immediate danger

New Zealand　　Shine Helpline 0508-744-633

Visit: www.2shine.org.nz

United States　　National Domestic Violence Hotline

1-800-799-SAFE (7233)

1-800-787-3224 (TTY)

Advocates are also available to chat 24/7.

Canada　　　　Dial 911 if in immediate danger

Shelter Safe: info@endvaw.ca

United Kingdom　National Centre for Domestic Violence

0800 970 2070 or text "NCDV" to 60777
and get a callback

ncdv.org.uk

Printed in Great Britain
by Amazon

83379997R00088